1985

The Scott, Foresman PROC

Series Editors

Roderick P. Hart
University of Texas at Austin

Ronald L. Applbaum
Pan American University

Titles in the PROCOM Series

THE GUIDE TO BETTER COMMUNICATION IN GOVERNMENT SERVICE
Raymond L. Falcione
In consultation with James G. Dalton

THE MILITARY OFFICER'S GUIDE TO BETTER COMMUNICATION
L. Brooks Hill
In consultation with Major Michael Gallagher

THE NURSE'S GUIDE TO BETTER COMMUNICATION
Robert E. Carlson
In consultation with Margaret Kidwell Udin and Mary Carlson

THE PHYSICIAN'S GUIDE TO BETTER COMMUNICATION
Barbara F. Sharf
In consultation with Dr. Joseph A. Flaherty

THE POLICE OFFICER'S GUIDE TO BETTER COMMUNICATION
T. Richard Cheatham
Keith V. Erickson
In consultation with Frank Dyson

PROFESSIONALLY SPEAKING
A Concise Guide
Robert J. Doolittle
In consultation with Thomas Towers

For further information, write to

Professional Publishing Group
Scott, Foresman and Company
1900 East Lake Avenue
Glenview, IL 60025

Professionally Speaking

A Concise Guide

Robert J. Doolittle, Ph.D.
University of Wisconsin, Milwaukee

In consultation with
Thomas Towers
Northwestern Mutual Life Insurance Company

Scott, Foresman and Company   Glenview, Illinois
Dallas, Texas   Oakland, New Jersey   Palo Alto, California
Tucker, Georgia   London

Library of Congress Cataloging in Publication Data

Doolittle, Robert J.
  Professionally speaking.

  Includes bibliographical references and index.
  1. Public speaking.   I. Towers, Thomas.   II. Title.
PN4121.D73   1984   808.5'1   83-20171
ISBN 0-673-15548-X

1 2 3 4 5 6 7 — MAL — 88 87 86 85 84 83

CONTENTS

On Becoming an Effective Public Person   1

CHAPTER 1

The Fear of Public Communication: Monsters of the Mind   5

CHAPTER 2

Before You Say a Word: Thinking About Public Talk   19

FOREWORD

This volume is part of a series entitled *ProCom* (Professional Communication), which has been created to bring the very latest thinking about human communication to the attention of working professionals. Busy professionals rarely have time for theoretical writings on communication oriented toward general readers, and the books in the ProCom series have been designed to provide the information they need. This volume and the others in the series focus on what communication scholars have learned recently that might prove useful to professionals, how certain principles of interaction can be applied in concrete situations, and what difference the latest thoughts about communication can make in the lives and careers of professionals.

Most professionals want to improve their communication skills in the context of their unique professional callings. They don't want pie-in-the-sky solutions divorced from the reality of their jobs. And, because they are professionals, they typically distrust uninformed advice offered by uninformed advisors, no matter how well intentioned the advice and the advisors might be.

The books in this series have been carefully adapted to the needs and special circumstances of modern professionals. For example, it becomes obvious that the skills needed by a nurse when communicating with the family of a terminally ill patient will differ markedly from those demanded of an attorney when coaxing crucial testimony out of a reluctant witness. Furthermore, analyzing the nurse's or attorney's experiences will hardly help an engineer explain a new bridge's stress fractures to state legislators, a military officer motivate a group of especially dispirited recruits, or a police officer calm a vicious domestic disturbance. All these situations require a special kind of professional with a special kind of professional training. It is ProCom's intention to supplement that training in the area of communication skills.

Each of the authors of the ProCom volumes has extensively taught, written about, and listened to professionals in his or her area. In addition, the books have profited from the services of area consultants—working professionals who have practical experience with the special kinds of communication problems that confront their co-workers. The authors and the area consultants have collaborated to provide solutions to these vexing problems.

We, the editors of the series, believe that ProCom will treat you well. We believe that you will find no theory-for-the-sake-of-theory here. We believe that you will find a sense of expertise. We believe that you will find the content of the ProCom volumes to be specific rather than general, concrete rather than abstract, applied rather than theoretical. We believe that you will find the examples interesting, the information appropriate, and the applications useful. We believe that you will find the ProCom volumes helpful whether you read them on your own or use them in a workshop. We know that ProCom has brought together the most informed authors and the best analysis and advice possible. We ask you to add your own professional goals and practical experiences so that your human communication holds all the warmth that makes it human and all the clarity that makes it communication.

Roderick P. Hart
University of Texas at Austin

Ronald L. Applbaum
Pan American University

PREFACE

Effective public communication has long been viewed as both a problem and an opportunity by professional people. It is a problem because it demands understandings and skills which were not a part of the education and training of many professionals, and because it places demands on the time and energies of people with other serious responsibilities. It is an opportunity that few professionals can ignore because it is often the most effective means of responding to a variety of needs, concerns, and expectations. The ability to be effective in a variety of public communication situations is essential to the successful manager, director, executive, or professional person.

Unfortunately, professional people too often approach public communication situations with insufficient understanding, inadequate preparation, and considerable trepidation. The results are just as often uncomfortable and unsatisfactory. The perspective of *Professionally Speaking* is that professional people can learn to be effective public persons. A concise yet systematic approach is provided here to permit you to develop your abilities to prepare, present, and evaluate public messages.

Substantial space is devoted to the thinking and planning processes which precede the preparation of public speeches. Included in this discussion are specific suggestions about how to decide when it is better *not* to speak publicly. Each aspect of message preparation is reviewed, and specific instructions for rehearsal and presentation are provided. A unique and proven method for managing manuscript presentations is presented as well. Finally, an entire chapter is devoted to techniques for responding to questions from audiences and from representatives of the media.

Simply reading *Professionally Speaking* will not guarantee that you will become an effective public communicator. Public speaking is a mobile skill; it must be practiced to be improved. This book will help you to understand what effective public communication requires so that you can prepare and practice well, evaluate what you do, and improve with each presentation.

This book is the result of many efforts. Rod Hart persuaded me that it was worth doing and encouraged me at critical points. Ron Applbaum offered useful comments and ran deft interference for me. Professor Melvin Miller, my colleague and jogging partner at the University of Wisconsin, Milwaukee, offered encouragement, examples, and timely criticisms of my writing. Barbara Kuster, Rosie Cacace, and Mary Jorgensen moved handwritten sheets into readable pages with speed, skill, and patience. Anita Portugal made the editorial process a pleasant experience. Tom Towers of Northwestern Mutual Life read this manuscript carefully and offered practical advice. Finally, my clients in the Milwaukee area have provided me with important insights into the problems and challenges which professional people confront daily. I have profited especially from my work with Fred Cashmore of the Wisconsin Telephone Company. Fred first suggested and then encouraged the development of the quarter-sheet manuscript format.

Public communication has been taught since the beginnings of recorded history. Always it has been seen as an essential tool to those who engage in business, commerce, politics, and practical affairs. Today, the person skilled in public communication is valued in all professions. If you are prepared to learn and apply what is offered here, you will discover that public communication situations offer more opportunities and fewer problems.

Robert J. Doolittle

On Becoming an Effective Public Person

Richard Sennett is a provocative, exasperating man. In 1974 he published *The Fall of Public Man*,[1] which the *New York Times* called "original and courageous" but also "troubling."[2] Throughout his book Sennett argues that a "state of decay" has set in in public life because of the blurring of the necessary distinction between "public" and "private" life. Speaking about Americans, Sennett maintains that we are losing our ability to interact effectively in public with those we do not know well; increasingly, we want "community" and "fraternity," and to get it we have retreated from public encounters in a "modern, urban society of strangers," preferring instead to deal with those we know and with whom we share common values.

The temptation to reject Sennett's indictment is almost overwhelming. As educators, business people, public servants, and citizens of a democracy, we would like to believe that we are competent public persons as well as effective private persons. We would like to believe, contrary to Sennett's intemperate accusations, that we can interact with strangers as effectively as with intimates. Unfortunately, however, there is too much evidence to support Sennett, especially in examining the propensities of professional people. To elaborate:

PUBLIC COMMUNICATION IS YOUR RESPONSIBILITY

For some ten years now, I have served as a public communication consultant to business and professional people. My clients have included company presidents, chief executive officers, and major public officials. With rare exceptions, my task in teaching public communication skills is complicated early on by an underlying distaste for and fear of public encounters on the part of these professional people. On the one hand, they will reluctantly acknowledge the need for making public appearances and public presentations; on the other hand, they will resist—sometimes vocally—the idea that such public communication is their *personal* responsibility. Expressions like "This [public communication] is the least attractive part of my job" or "There have to be people in this organization who are better equipped to do this" are common. Such comments suggest that otherwise competent professional people assume that, while public communication competency may be nice for some, it is not necessary for them. Or they assume that public communication competency is reserved for a select group of people who will serve as spokespersons on their behalf.

If further evidence is needed of the public reticence of professional people, one need only read David Finn's stinging attack on corporate leaders in a recent issue of the *Harvard Business Review*. In an article entitled "Public Invisibility of Corporate Leaders," Finn lays much of the blame for U.S. business's persistently low score in public opinion surveys on "the failure of corporate executives to convincingly present themselves as persons who truly care about the state of the world in which they live." Indeed, Finn notes, executives who exercise their skills as public communicators are often criticized by colleagues and competitors for "making speeches and seeking the limelight."[3]

In a similar vein, Robert V. Krikorian, vice-chairman and chief executive officer of Rexnord, Inc., urges business people to speak out to overcome the facelessness of American business: "Countless of us are realizing that public appearances to discuss the shared problems of society and business are integral to our jobs."[4] This book is concerned with developing public communication competency. But, of necessity, it is first concerned with the task of convincing professional people of the need for and value of becoming competent public persons.

BECOME EFFECTIVE *PUBLIC PERSONS*

It should be painfully evident to professional people that they are public persons, whether they wish to be or not. They are public persons because of increasing public scrutiny of previously "private" businesses, corporations, industries, and government agencies. In recent years consumer interest in corporate and government activity, together with the aggressive pursuit by media of the public's right to know, has blurred the distinction between private and public activity. Such intensive and often hostile scrutiny demands that professional people be prepared to speak clearly and effectively in a variety of public forums and through various media. This is the era of the consumer. To survive and thrive in it, professional people must be capable of effective public communication in response to public demands—especially when those demands are ill-informed, distorted, unjustified; or make no sense at all.

Increasing government regulation of private enterprise requires that professional people develop their skills as public persons. Virtually every aspect of professional and private activity is monitored by a host of local, state, and federal agencies: the IRS, ICC, FTC, EPA, EOC—the litany of familiar regulating acronyms goes on and on. Most professional people would readily agree that there is a critical need to respond in articulate and effective ways to government regulators—even to the point of publicly protesting the trend toward overregulation.

A public person must be a competent communicator if the challenges posed by consumers and government are to be met, but there are other compelling and personal reasons why professional people need to become competent public communicators. For example, there is increasing evidence that hiring and promotion decisions at the managerial level are often strongly influenced by demonstrated public communication capability.[5] This does not mean that other job skills are not as important as public communication competence, but it does mean that, other factors being equal or nearly equal, public communication skill will be the *single most influential factor* determining a hiring or promotion decision. A recent survey of over 2,200 employers showed that effective public communication skills are the single most sought-after skills in new employees.[6] Business, industrial, and other organizations prosper or die in direct proportion to the efficiency and effectiveness of both internal and external communication. It is hardly surprising, then, that employees who are competent public communicators are increasingly valued and rewarded in the workplace.

Finally, professional people—perhaps more than any other group in the country—need to be effective public persons because our form of government demands it. This democratic society was predicated on a vision of an informed and articulate citizenry. It cannot survive if its citizens fail their responsibilities to become informed and to speak up publicly. The most dangerous aspect of the "silent majority" is its damnable silence. Professional people are assumed to be—rightly so—leaders of their communities. If they will not or cannot exert public leadership through effective public communication, then their communities and ultimately the nation suffer. This fact is well understood in board rooms and business offices. Corporations, businesses, and industries have in recent years begun to encourage greater community involvement by all employees, from chief executive officers to mail clerks.[7]

Richard Sennett's troublesome indictment is worth remembering.

We recognize easily enough the necessity of developing our skills as private persons. We need to develop our abilities to communicate effectively with intimates, family members, friends, and colleagues. What is too often overlooked and neglected is the equally urgent need to be effective with those who are not well known to us. The public person is one who actively seeks a full public life, who recognizes the responsibilities and rewards of being an effective public person, and who continually seeks to be effective in a variety of situations—with individuals and with large audiences.

This book is devoted to assisting you in your efforts to become an effective public person. But conviction and commitment come first. You must recognize the personal urgency of being an effective public communicator, and you must be prepared to do what is necessary to achieve such effectiveness. As a mature individual, as a professional person, and as a leading citizen, you must ask yourself if you can afford not to be an effective public person.

Notes

1. Sennett, R., *The Fall of Public Man* (New York: Alfred A. Knopf, 1977).

2. Wolin, S., "The Rise of Private Man," review of *The Fall of Public Man*, by Richard Sennett, *New York Review of Books*, 1977, no. 24: 19–26.

3. Finn, D., "Public Invisibility of Corporate Leaders," *Harvard Business Review* (November–December 1980): 102–10.

4. Krikorian, R. V., *The Bridge to Public Trust* (Milwaukee: Rexnord, 1980).

5. A host of studies confirming the importance of oral communication training for business and professional persons have been reported in recent years. For example, see McBath, J. H., & Burbans, D. T., Jr., *Communication Education for Careers* (Falls Church, Va.: Speech Communication Association, 1975): 57–64; Endicott, F. S., *The Endicott Report, 1980: Employment Trends for College Graduates* (Evanston, Ill.: Northwestern University, 1980); Page, P., & Perlman, S., *Basic Skills and Employment: An Employer Survey* (Madison: University of Wisconsin System Office of Academic Affairs, 1980).

6. Hagge-Greenberge, L., *Report on the Liberal Arts Employer Survey: Opportunities for the Liberal Arts Graduate* (Oberlin, Ohio: Midwest College Placement Association Liberal Arts Group, 1979).

7. Morrison, A. M., "The Boss as Pitchman," *Fortune* (August 1980): 66–73.

CHAPTER 1

The Fear of Public Communication: Monsters of the Mind

Some years ago, the United States Armed Forces Radio Network in Europe carried live a remarkable broadcast of a Halloween hoax. An unsuspecting reporter was sent to a deserted castle in Bavaria, which, he was told, was rumored to be the estate of the infamous Dr. Frankenstein. He was to do a live broadcast from the cellar of the old castle near midnight as a Halloween feature. He was not told that he was the target of an elaborate practical joke. The cellar room from which he was to broadcast had been ingeniously rigged to reveal a "Frankenstein monster" at the appropriate moment, and the monster would appear to move. The reporter had been supplied with a flashlight with weak batteries that failed early in the broadcast.

The joke worked well—too well. The hapless reporter opened the broadcast with lively patter about the Frankenstein myth and the reputed history of the castle. As he stumbled around in the cellar, he periodically assured his listeners that it was all fiction and that they, and he, had nothing to fear—nothing at all to fear. Then, as the light from his flashlight faded, he discovered the likeness of the Frankenstein monster planted in the cellar by his mischievous colleagues. His composure began to slip badly. He gasped. Quickly he explained that he had been caught off guard when he stumbled onto the monster. There was, he said, nothing to be afraid of; it was merely a statue, a likeness—or something. It was all very silly, but the thing *was* hideous. Then, as he began to describe the monster, it was made to move by remote control. At that point, his uneasy rationalizations collapsed completely; he dashed for a door only to find it locked. Then, with listeners all over Europe hanging on every sound, he became hysterical and fainted. In the background, a dog barked piteously. Thus ended a cruel practical joke which brought recriminations for months.

FEAR OF PUBLIC SPEAKING

The case is intriguing because it illustrates in a particularly dramatic way how fear can be made overwhelming by efforts to rationalize it away. The more that reporter talked about how he was not afraid, the more fearful he became. In less dramatic but nevertheless unmistakable ways, I believe professional people seriously mismanage their fear of public communication. Few professional people will openly admit to fear of public communication, but their verbal and other behaviors provide evidence of strong and occasionally incapacitating fear of public speaking.

This chapter, then, focuses on the fear of public communication. Such fear is found in all walks of life as well as among well-educated, competent professional people. *The Book of Lists* reported an impressively large survey among Americans in which respondents were asked to rank-order the things they feared most. The overwhelming majority of respondents listed "giving a public speech" as the thing they feared most. Death was a distant sixth on the same list![1]

In my work as a public communication consultant, I have heard corporate officers and public officials recount episodes of sweaty palms, shaking knees, disorientation, and nausea prior to and during public communication efforts. Interestingly, such accounts are frequently preceded by such disclaimers as "I don't think I'm afraid of public speaking, but . . ." or "This kind of thing never happened to me before, but. . . ." Often efforts are quickly made to explain away such reactions by reference to too little sleep, a heavy meal, a hot room, or preoccupation with other—presumably more substantial—worries.[2]

I have been intrigued, too, with the increasing popularity in recent years of self-improvement workshops for corporate executives. These workshops, which focus primarily on instilling confidence and overcoming stage fright, characteristically avoid direct mention of fear. Rather, they offer training in "assertiveness," "image building," and "self-control" in public communication. And corporate officers happily pay fees exceeding $1,000 a day for such training. It is as if admitting to fear of public communication—even to oneself—is too onerous for professional people to contemplate. Indeed, major corporate officers often appear to feel they are *less* entitled to express fear of public speaking than their less publicly responsive subordinates.

Fear Can Be Helpful

The perspective offered here is that such belabored denials of fear of public communication are unnecessary, unhealthy, and unproductive. Fear of public speaking is widespread, real, and potentially helpful in developing public communication skills. Like that hapless reporter in "Frankenstein's castle," the more we attempt to deny or explain away our fears of public communication, the more we are apt to create "monsters" in our minds that will inhibit our abilities as effective public communicators. By admitting and confronting such fear, we can discover its causes and the means to control it and turn it to our advantage.

Fear Results from What We Do Not Know

When we confront the fear of public communication, we make a startling discovery. Like other fears, our fear of public speaking is largely the result of what we do not know or what is poorly understood and distorted. Our ignorance and misconceptions of public communication, more than anything else, feed our fears and prevent our development as effective public communicators. Widespread fear of public communication has three common elements: First, professional people and others are plagued by serious ignorance of the nature of public communication. We know too little about the fundamental assumptions and requirements of the public communication process. So myths and misconceptions abound. Second, the lack of formal training in public communication leads too frequently to botched and embarrassing experiences with public communication, further confirming our worst fears of public encounters. Finally, professionals and others too often are unable to assess their public communication experiences—the successes as well as the failures. We know too little about why some public communication encounters seem to succeed and satisfy and why others fail miserably. Our inability to assess public communication experiences makes it impossible for us to improve public communication effectiveness through informed and constructive criticism. Each new public speaking encounter carries the same ambiguities and hazards that characterized all those in the past.

The remainder of this chapter will consequently focus on providing a better understanding of public communication as a prelude to more effective preparation and more informed and constructive assessment of public communication encounters. We will look at the fundamental assumptions and requirements of public communication, and we will attack the myths and misconceptions that exacerbate our fears of public communication. Before beginning that discussion, however, it will be useful to examine the physical and psychological manifestations of stage fright or the fear of public speaking. Once we understand *how* it operates, we will be better able to understand *why* it occurs and what can be done to control and utilize it.

Fear Is Both Physical and Psychological

The fear of public communication is both physical and psychological. The physical manifestations may include a dry mouth, difficulty in swallowing, shortness of breath, and a host of other unpleasant sensations. Confronted by a tense or threatening situation, the human body reacts by increasing the secretion of adrenalin. Our pulse rate increases, we breathe faster, and our digestive processes slow down so that blood and oxygen will be more available to the brain and large muscles. We are likely to feel an emptiness in our stomach and a little light-headed. This reaction to the tensions induced by public speaking situations can, if not controlled, become self-generating and increasingly unpleasant. We may become more tense as we experience the results of an increased secretion of adrenalin. Our increased tenseness results in even more adrenalin, followed by heightened tension. If unchecked, this process would continue until we passed out.

Fortunately, most public communicators are able to control their tenseness somewhere short of fainting. All public speakers, however, experience some stage fright, some nervousness as their bodies react to the threat or challenge of public communication. Experienced and knowledgeable public speakers have learned to control and utilize the extra energy that increased adrenalin provides. In Chapter 5 we will review specific techniques which will help you control the physical reactions to public speaking. Like experienced speakers, you can learn to anticipate, use, and even welcome such reactions. Part of that control comes from knowing what is happening to your body as you prepare to speak and as you speak.

The psychological aspects of stage fright are more difficult to describe because they are more subjective and variable. Some people seem especially daring; others are frightened by their shadows. We are all to some personal extent fearful of the unknown. I marveled, as did most moviegoers, at the incredible daring of Indiana Jones, the hero of the movie *Raiders of the Lost Ark*. And I noticed that some people closed their eyes during critical portions of the story. Similarly, some people are more fearful than others as they confront the uncertainties and risks of public speaking. And some speakers who are comfortable in some public speaking occasions may feel especially threatened in others.

In all public communication we confront an array of personal concerns, which, taken together, will account for our fear of such situations. We are, for example, concerned about how people will react to us and to what we have to say. Will they like us? Believe us? See us as competent? With some audiences and some messages and some situations we are confident, even bold. With other audiences, messages, and situations we are confident, even bold. With other audiences, messages, and situations we are unsure and fearful. Some years ago I assisted a public figure who felt supremely confident when talking to large, general audiences. With smaller, special-interest groups, however, he was hesitant, fearful, and reticent. As he learned to predict their reactions to his messages with greater precision, his confidence in such encounters improved. We all should know as best we can how people will react to us in a variety of public encounters. In Chapter 3 we will learn specific ways of doing just that.

Even with familiar audiences we may experience some apprehension as we review the extent of our preparation. When we have prepared well we tend to be more confident. When we are not fully prepared, we find it difficult to avoid that nasty gremlin in our head who seems to delight in reminding us of our shortcomings. We will see in the remaining chapters how to prepare completely and how to convince ourselves of the adequacy of our preparation.

It should be clear: fear of public communication is the direct result of ignorance and uncertainty. We need to understand and anticipate the physical manifestations of stage fright. We need to understand the psychological concerns that influence our fear of public speaking and learn how we can address those concerns through careful preparation. Careful preparation, however, assumes that we first understand the fundamental assumptions and requirements of public communication. An examination of the assumptions of public communication will help us understand *why* we often fear public communication. And an examination of the requirements of public communication will serve to direct our preparation for and our critical assessment of public speaking.

·

MUTUAL RISKS

Public communication assumes mutual risks. When a speaker addresses an audience, the speaker confronts personal risks and his or her audience accepts personal and collective risks. Most public communicators are keenly aware of their personal risks in public encounters—one major cause of their fears. They understand intuitively, for example, that they will be judged for what they say and how they say it. Their personal competence, expertise, and integrity will be judged by members of the audience. The speaker will reveal personal values, attitudes, and visions, and those too will be judged. When you speak you risk your credibility as a person and as a public speaker. It is small wonder that some politicians regularly evade public speaking invitations.

There is, however, another major area of risk for public speakers. When we speak, we speak for a specific purpose. We want people to understand something, believe something, or act on something. Each time we speak, then, we risk failure in achieving our purpose. The audience may misunderstand or distort what we say. They may disagree with our position and become even more difficult to persuade in subsequent efforts. They may react in a hostile way, subjecting us to ridicule and sarcasm. They may refuse to act as we request. No one likes to fail, and *public* failure is even more humiliating. The risks of public communication are all too real, so we do well to consider those risks carefully before venturing into public forums.

What is often not so clearly understood by public speakers are the collective and personal risks that audience members accept. Speakers, of course, offer everything from eternal life to hair restoratives to economic salvation; audience members risk exposing themselves to such messages. This is to say nothing of the time expended by audience members attending to public messages. Listeners are no more anxious to waste time than are speakers.

Beyond this obvious risk, public audiences run other risks. They risk accepting and empathizing with public speakers even when they do not accept fully the ideas, products, or behaviors those speakers offer. Early polls, for example, revealed that Americans admired and liked Ronald Reagan even though the same polls showed sharp disagreement with his economic and, especially, foreign policies. Nevertheless, Mr. Reagan's personal popularity was skillfully used as a mandate for sweeping changes in economic, military, and foreign policies.

The risks that audience members run are all too evident to them. Listeners may even regard their risks in public encounters as disproportionately large, compared to the risks that speakers run. To illustrate this for yourself simply recount the reasons you used to turn down a "free" dinner to be followed by a pitch for real estate in Florida or Colorado. Effective public communicators must be sensitive to the risks they confront and those they impose on their listeners. Their efforts must then be directed toward reducing their risks *and* the risks of their listeners.

MUTUAL CONTROL

Public communication further assumes mutual control. Public communicators easily recognize the need to control listeners in public encounters. At the least, a public speaker expects to attract and hold the attention of his or her listeners for some period of time. The speaker expects to exert enough control over the audience to have his or her message heard without significant interruption. Beyond this, of course, speakers expect to direct the perceptions and understandings of listeners, introduce new ideas, change existing ideas, and manage behavior. All of this suggests efforts by the public speaker to control the audience.

For many, the notion that public speaking requires control of listeners is distastefully heavy-handed. It smacks of manipulation, exploitation, and—at worst—deception. Such a reaction is understandable but clearly short-sighted. If speakers had no interest in controlling the responses of listeners, there would be no justification in attempting public speech. And control in public exchange is not unilateral. In inescapable ways the public communicator is controlled by the audience. Let's examine an example of public communication to see how both the speaker and the listeners are controlled.

In the Introduction, I referred to remarks made by Robert V. Krikorian at the annual Peter E. Rentscher Memorial Lecture before the Iron Castings Society. Even a cursory examination of this event suggests that Mr. Krikorian was controlled by the audience he confronted on that September morning. This was a formal occasion with a specific history and a clear function. The Rentscher lecture is the major speech delivered before the annual convention and meeting of the society; the audience is composed of business executives concerned about foundry operations and about general business issues that affect their industry and others. If Mr. Krikorian was to be effective before such a group, he needed to identify his ideas with these overriding concerns. To speak of his interest in sports, to champion his favorite political candidates, or even to discuss problems unique to his own company would have been clearly inappropriate. He was controlled in his selection of a topic and his means of discussing that topic.

Because it was a formal occasion, Mr Krikorian was further controlled in his manner of presenting the lecture. Memorial lectures typically are recorded, printed, and widely distributed. They often become part of the historical records kept by professional societies. Further, there are definite time expectations and limitations associated with such public speeches. These, too, controlled the public behavior of Mr. Krikorian on that occasion. For him to deliver a few casual remarks "off the cuff" would clearly have violated the expectations of his listeners.

Certainly, Robert Krikorian had specific views to convey and specific responses he wished to elicit from those listeners. But he recognized, as must all public communicators, that he could succeed in his purposes only if he accepted the demands which *that* situation and *those* receivers made upon him. This example, of course, does not begin to exhaust the ways by which speakers and audiences manage to control each other in public situations; but it does perhaps clarify the issue. Mutual control is an inescapable feature of public communication encounters. In *Behavior in Public Places*, Erving Goffman examines in fascinating detail how the issue of "social control" is defined and negotiated in public interchange.[3] Those who aspire to become consistently effective public communicators will find Goffman's work instructive. Those who are made uncomfortable by the notion of mutual control in public communication should consider this book required reading.

MUTUAL BENEFIT

Finally, public communication assumes mutual benefits. Without some promise of reward there would be no reason to accept the risks inherent in public encounters. Speakers of course expect to benefit from their public communication efforts. The rewards of public speaking are easily enumerated. The speaker's public image may be enhanced. Audiences may readily acknowledge their acceptance of the speaker's credibility. Anyone who has been publicly applauded knows how rewarding public acknowledgment can be. The speaker may be amply rewarded in simply accomplishing—even partially—the purposes that occasioned the engagement. When our ideas are understood, our beliefs adopted, our visions shared, our products bought, and our recommended courses of action followed, we experience the rewards of public communication. Public speakers may also be rewarded by being given more opportunities for public communication. These rewards individually and collectively provide the motivation to face the risks and demands of public communication again and again.

Public communication fails, however, if audience members perceive the encounter as insufficiently rewarding. Simply put, audiences demand from the outset that public speakers make each public communication encounter worth their time and involvement. What is a "sufficient" reward for a public audience? The only acceptable answer: whatever they feel they are entitled to receive, given their interests and concerns and what they feel their involvement is worth in a given public communication event.

Calculating specifically what an audience will demand for themselves in a public communication encounter is a little like trying to calculate the salary necessary to entice a professional athlete to sign and honor a long-term contract. What are the prevailing costs? The payoffs for audiences, like those for public speakers, are varied. They may include satisfaction of personal and collective needs for information and enlightenment, reduction of ambiguity, resolution of problems, assurances of safety and security, and respite from boredom. Whatever audiences require, the speaker must attempt to anticipate and provide it or face failure.

Public communication assumes *mutual* benefits, not necessarily *equal* benefits. In some encounters, the speaker may profit handsomely compared to what rewards the audience receives; in other encounters, audience members will benefit more than the speaker. Only one thing is certain: A public speaker will be rewarded by an audience only if and to the extent they see their reasonable demands for rewards satisfied.

Public communication is an activity that assumes mutual risks, mutual control, and mutual benefit. Understanding this can direct our preparation for public speaking, assist our efforts to evaluate our public communication efforts, and relieve our fears of public encounters.

MYTHS ABOUT PUBLIC COMMUNICATION

As I suggested earlier in this chapter, our fears of public speaking result not only from what we do not know or understand about public communication but also from misconceptions and myths about public encounters. These misconceptions and myths persist among professional people as well as the general public. Let us turn now to an examination of these persistent myths about public communication, which, like our ignorance and misunderstandings of the fundamental assumptions and requirements of public speaking, exacerbate our fears and prevent our development as competent public persons.

Myth: Public Speaking Is a Special Activity

Perhaps the most common and doggedly persistent myth about public communication is that it is a "special" activity reserved for unusual occasions. There is even a commonsense argument that appears to support this myth. After all, the argument goes, how often do you make a public speech? There are only a few special occasions during the year when even an outgoing professional person will step behind a podium to give a public speech, and many professional people can count on one hand the number of public speeches given in a career. Surely, then, public communication is a rare activity reserved for especially important occasions.

This argument, of course, ignores the true nature of public communication and the nature of the occasions in which it occurs. Richard Sennett's notion of the public person is one who "connects with strangers in an emotionally satisfying way."[4] Sennett argues that public communication is, or shoud be, a regular feature of daily living. When we engage with people we do not know well to solve problems, share understanding and perspectives, advocate points of view, or seek stimulation, we are engaged in public speaking. Roderick P. Hart, Gustav Friedrich, and William Brooks provide further definition of "public occasions":

> Such occasions (1) are usually planned in advance, (2) are guided by an
> agenda of activity, (3) have an allocation of management functions (some

person or persons perform standard roles and do certain things), (4) have clear-cut and agreed-on specifications of what constitutes proper and improper conduct, and (5) conform to a preestablished unfolding of phases— certain things are done at certain times."[5]

Certainly, even this specification of the nature of the "special occasions" for public communication reveals it as familiar, daily activity that transpires in the streets, in restaurants, in board rooms, courtrooms, parks, offices, factories, and PTA meetings. Donald K. Smith puts it succinctly: "There is no fundamental discontinuity between the necessities, opportunities, and problems of the public speaker, and those confronted by every person using speech in the conduct of his daily affairs."[6]

Is public speaking an unusual activity reserved for special occasions and restricted to the lectern or platform? Hardly. Rather it is, and should be developed as, an everyday activity occurring in any location where people come together. Public communication responds to the needs, problems, and opportunities that confront people daily. It is, as Sennett suggests, an expected and frequent activity for the public person—an inescapable feature of public life.

Myth: The Public Speaker Is Especially Gifted

A related misconception about public communication which sets the knees of professional people to trembling is the belief that the public speaker is a specially gifted individual with innate abilities and God-given propensities. While most professional people would reject as silly the idea that public speakers are born, not made, they nevertheless often feel that the effective public communicator has developed unusual personal talents to a remarkable degree. The term "public speaker" conjures up images of such polished and charismatic public figures as Ronald Reagan, Ted Kennedy, William Buckley, Barbara Jordan, and Gloria Steinem. And too many people are defeated by those images. At the heart of this misconception—like the myth of public speaking as a "special" activity—is an overly narrow view of what a public person is and does.

Development as an effective public communicator begins with the understanding that you need not be a nationally known, speak-for-pay, professional platform speaker to be a competent public person. The public communicator is most often *not* a charismatic, flamboyant spellbinder with a million-dollar vocabulary who speaks the King's English perfectly and is capable of a glib if not meaningful response in all public settings. Bruce Gronbeck offers a more realistic and manageable vision of the public speaker: "Most audiences in America today are not looking for silver-tongued spellbinders; they are seeking sympathetic, understanding persons of integrity. Verbal gymnasts, of course, still have their places at political conventions, in revivalist halls, and on used car lots; but most of us will not speak publicly at those sites."[7] The public speaker is an ordinary person who confronts the necessity of being a public person and uses common abilities to meet the fundamental assumptions and requirements of daily public encounters.

Myth: Public Speeches Are Chiseled in Rock

A less widespread but serious misconception of public speaking is reflected in the belief that public speeches are "made for the ages." A public speech is sometimes viewed as a historical event which will be a part of a continuing and generally available public record. As with most myths, there is an element of truth here. Speakers do indeed "stand with" their public utterances, and the audience members may indeed remember for some time what was said. And some public speeches are faithfully recorded, transcribed, reproduced, and made a part of broadly available historical records. But those instances are rare compared to the thousands of unrecorded public speeches made each day.

The trouble is that if we assume that everything we say in public will be recorded, remembered, broadly disseminated, and dredged up at some later time when it will appear inadequate, wrong, or irrelevant, we would probably say very little publicly. We are rarely so absolutely sure of what we say publicly that we would have it chiseled in rock. There is little justification in such an assumption.

Public communication is usually situation-specific and ephemeral. Most audiences do well if they remember as much as 40 percent of what a speaker·says immediately after the speaker concludes; even less is retained as time goes by. This fact is both reassuring and challenging to the public communicator. On the one hand, it suggests that there is room for human error in making public pronouncements; on the other hand, it challenges the public speaker to be as informed as possible and to strive through careful preparation and skillful organization of public messages to defeat the poor listening habits of most public audiences.

Effective public communicators understand that public discourse is instrumental. That is, it strives to accomplish a specific goal with a specific audience at a specific time. To be fully realized, some speaker goals will require a series of messages over time with a particular audience or many audiences. Indeed, the major goal of some public speeches is to create opportunities for further public messages. Public messages are routinely made, later enlarged, still later corrected and reframed, and continuously revised. So long as human knowledge is imperfect and incomplete, there will be in public speaking—as in all human activity—room for error. Public communication is significant activity; it is remembered and, occasionally, made a part of literature and history. But that should not be a cause for refraining from public speaking lest we err in some small or large way.

Myth: Public Speaking Is an Exact Science

Finally, professional people perhaps more than other groups often subscribe to the misconception that public communication must be an exact science, that if it is done properly it will succeed. The troublesome corollary to this reasoning is that if public communication fails, it has to be because it was improperly prepared and executed. This argument suggests a formulistic and rigidly scientific vision of the nature of the preparation for and delivery of public messages, and it imposes an oppressive responsibility on the makers of public messages. Further it blithely ignores the vagaries of human interaction. Public speakers achieve their goals *through* their listeners, and the only truly predictable aspect of human listeners is their unpredictability. Further, public messages may succeed despite inadequate preparation and dreadful delivery.

Those who aspire to be competent public persons need to understand that there are no surefire formulas to success as public speakers. There are only understandings, principles, and techniques that offer an improved likelihood of success in most public encounters. Some of our most carefully prepared, artistically adapted, and masterfully delivered public communication efforts will fail—for no damned good reason at all! The mature public person soon realizes that failure is inevitable and instructive.

It is the serendipitous success that is to be most dreaded. A "lucky" but undeserved success leaves us only momentary gain, the feeling that we have escaped our just desserts, and gnawing concern for how we will manage the next public encounter. A well-understood failure, on the other hand, can assist us to identify and correct shortcomings in our preparation and delivery of public messages. They are a spur to insightful analysis and growth—and, from time to time, a healthy reminder that we live in an imperfect world.

This chapter began with the assertion that professional people mismanage their fears of public communication. Much of that fear is unnecessarily self-induced; it results from our ignorance of what public communication assumes and demands and from our misconceptions of the nature of public speaking. Once we understand what public encounters assume and demand, once we unburden ourselves of the myths that handicap our growth as public persons, we can begin to prepare ourselves for public speaking confident in the knowledge that our preparation is soundly based and offers the best hope for our development as competent public persons.

LEARNING TO BE YOUR OWN BEST CRITIC

If we begin properly, each public speaking experience becomes a major step toward becoming expert in the business of public speaking. Each public speech becomes an opportunity for analysis and constructive critique. Each public encounter allows us to examine the extent to which we have met fundamental assumptions and requirements and the extent to which we have managed the opportunities and obstacles inherent in those encounters. We will learn with ever-increasing precision to pinpoint our personal strengths and weaknesses, to become our own best critics. The difference between mere experience and "studied" experience lies in our abilities to understand and grow as a direct result of each new experience.

Effective public communication cannot be learned from a book—not even this book. Public speaking is a mobile skill; it is learned in the doing. The ability to improve our skills as public communicators depends upon our willingness to seek out public speaking opportunities and then to subject each of those opportunities to systematic and informed critical review. This book presumes to assist that process by offering the means of sound preparation and informed self-criticism.

SUMMARY

This chapter began by focusing upon the fear of public speaking. The argument of this chapter is that efforts to deny fear are unnecessary, unhealthy, and unproductive. If confronted and examined, the fear of public speaking becomes less monstrous than it often appears for most people. Examined carefully the fear of public speaking is demonstrably a matter of what we do not know and what we mistakenly believe about public communication encounters. In public communication encounters speaker and audience share risks, exert mutual control, and anticipate shared benefits. These understandings will guide the efforts, described in the following chapters, to prepare ourselves for and to assess the success of public communication encounters.

Notes

1. Wallechinsky, D., Wallace, I., and Wallace, A., *The Book of Lists* (New York: Bantam, 1971), 469.

2. Over the past five years, through the administration of more than 2,000 questionnaires that probe key attitudes toward public encounters, I have collected data about the fear of public communication. While individual results vary widely, the pattern is clear. Virtually every person completing such a

questionnaire has indicated attitudes and experiences that reflect fear of public speaking. In a surprising number of instances, this fear has been substantial enough to cause the respondent to avoid most public speaking opportunities.

3. Goffman, E., *Behavior in Public Places* (New York: Free Press, 1962).

4. Sennett, R., *The Fall of Public Man* (New York: Alfred A. Knopf, 1974).

5. Hart, R. P., Friedrich, G. W., and Brooks, W., *Public Communication* (New York: Harper and Row, 1975), 24.

6. Smith, D. K., *Man Speaking* (New York: Dodd, Mead, 1969), 20.

7. Gronbeck, B. E., *The Articulate Person*, 2nd ed. (Glenview, Ill.: Scott, Foresman, 1983), 4.

CHAPTER *2*

Before You Say a Word: Thinking About Public Talk

Winston Churchill was, throughout an illustrious public life, a prolific writer and speaker. He is reported to have said, "If you wish for me to speak for an hour, give me ten minutes to prepare. If, however, you want me to speak for ten minutes, give me a month." Churchill was reflecting what all good public speakers know: The more we expect a message to do in a short period of time, the longer we will need to prepare ourselves to make and deliver that message.

Professional people confront the necessity of packing a great deal of purpose and meaning into public messages that conform to serious time pressures. American audiences have very little patience with public messages that last more than thirty minutes. As a public communicator, you will find few opportunities to speak longer than that. Often you will face the difficulty of saying what you need and want to say in less time than you would like to have. Professional people are busy: daily schedules are filled, meeting agendas are crowded, and other matters are always pressing.

General audiences are often worse. They have, for good or ill, been conditioned by the electronic media to respond to messages lasting thirty seconds or less. Attention spans are short, and distractions are plentiful. While they will attend to longer messages on some few occasions, those occasions are increasingly rare. The person who would be an effective public communicator must accept the necessity of saying what needs to be said in the shortest possible time. To do that, more time and skill will be required for preparation prior to speaking.

This chapter focuses on the first critical steps in preparing to speak **19** publicly. It addresses the initial judgments that must be made when thinking about public communication. How can you determine whether or not there is sufficient reason to speak publicly? How do you decide when to speak, assuming there is good reason to do so? And how do you determine what can reasonably be accomplished in the time you will have to speak, assuming there is reason and opportunity for doing so. These are important first questions, which, if they are not raised and answered before other preparation begins, presage inadequate preparation and potentially perplexing failure in public encounters.

DECIDING WHETHER TO SPEAK

Perhaps the most difficult question to ask ourselves in thinking about public speaking is "Is this talk necessary?" It is difficult to ask precisely because we are likely to quickly answer "No" or "Yes" and then find rationalizations to confirm our predilections. Our fear of public speaking, our underestimation of the values of public speaking, our preoccupation with other matters, and even our indolence may provoke an automatic denial of the need to speak publicly. Each negative reply then makes the next opportunity for public discourse more difficult to identify and confirm, and what public communication skills we have developed quickly atrophy from lack of use.

On the other hand, our eagerness to test our mettle as public persons, our strong feelings about some problem or issue, or the pressures from colleagues, cohorts, and community members may provoke an ill-considered decision to speak publicly. The competent public communicator is capable of addressing these matters and then acting as is best determined by the personal, professional, and audience considerations.

Personal Considerations

Personal considerations may provide some justification for public communication. Our personal needs for self-identity, social recognition, status, and stimulation may be satisfied by public speaking. For the past six years, I have assisted the training of a cadre of volunteer speakers for the Wisconsin Telephone Company. In that work I have met a number of remarkably dedicated people. One of the most outstanding members of that group is a delightfully energetic man, Romie Obermeier, who as a member of the company's volunteer speakers panel, has given more than 600 talks, and he is still active even after suffering some physical disabilities. His goal before he retires, he says, is to raise his total to 750.

Why does Obermeier speak? Like other volunteer speakers in the program, he is not paid. He often ends his workday only to drive a hundred miles to present a talk. Advancement in the company is not a major consideration; the company uses a complex rating system that emphasizes job competency to determine promotions, and Romie freely admits that he is not interested in job promotion as he nears retirement. Why does Romie speak?

Recently Obermeier was honored by the company when his talks surpassed 600, and I asked him then why he had remained so active in the volunteer program. His answer was predictable: He enjoys talking before groups of people. He draws personal satisfaction from the belief that he is helping other people in some way, and he welcomes the satisfaction he receives from knowing that he has done a good job in representing the Wisconsin Telephone Company. Public speaking may be personally rewarding. Personal considerations can and should asist us in our efforts to decide whether or not to speak publicly, but they cannot and should not be the sole justifications for public communication.

Professional Considerations

Like personal considerations, professional needs, problems, and responsibilities provide justification for public speaking. A company executive is made president and assumes the responsibility of being the chief spokesperson for the company; an engineer who directed the development of a new piece of electronic equipment is asked to use specialized knowledge to interest potential buyers. Each day professional people respond to exigencies to speak publicly as a result of their specialized talents and the recognition that their expertise uniquely qualifies them for some public utterance. Such opportunities dare not be overlooked. But professional considerations are not themselves sufficient to justify public communication.

Audience Considerations

We may speak because audiences invite—even demand—public discourse. Romie Obermeier speaks often and well because he believes people need to hear what he has to say; and he has, in the direct expressions of gratitude to him following his talks, ample evidence that he is right. Martin Luther King, Jr., spoke widely and often because he believed Americans needed a new vision of race relations; on the night President Kennedy was assassinated Lyndon Johnson spoke simply and well because he correctly surmised that the American people needed to be assured that the country was not threatened; each day hundreds of public speeches are made that attempt to identify and relieve audience needs and problems.

Public speakers must occasionally convince audiences of the existence of needs, deficiencies, or opportunities before attempting to explain how they can be met, corrected, or exploited. Recently in Milwaukee, a city engineer supervising the routine resurfacing of a heavily traveled bridge discovered major structural defects, which in his judgment made the bridge unsafe even for restricted traffic. Milwaukee taxpayers were not eager, of course, to learn that another major construction project was necessary. But the engineer realized they needed to know that the bridge was unsafe; each day, busloads of school children crossed the bridge. To his credit, he spoke up and publicly called for the bridge to be closed to traffic, pending a thorough, state-supervised inspection and reconstruction. A major justification for initiating public discourse is to identify and respond to audience needs, problems, and opportunities. But audience-related reasons are not, of themselves, sufficient to justify public speaking.

The foregoing discussion is not intended to confuse. Rather, it is intended to challenge you to examine the various factors that must be considered when deciding whether or not to speak publicly. I noted earlier that the competent public communicator attempts to understand the complex interplay of justifications that invite or discourage public discourse. It is not enough, for example, to rely upon personal or professional reasons for speaking. That encourages egocentricity and pedantry.

In the previous chapter I noted that public communication assumes mutual benefit for audience and speaker. Personal or professional reasons may, indeed, appear compelling; but unless they can be tied to some identifiable audience exigency, they must be denied. The speaker who insists upon imposing personal or professional agendas on audiences without regard to their concerns risks repeated and deserved failure. A simple but useful definition of effective public speaking is that it is a matter of getting others to understand, believe, or act as you wish them to—but for *their* reasons.

The notion that public discourse is justified solely by audience needs and desires is mistaken. The definition of a demagogue is one who uncritically panders to popular needs and prejudices. We may gain some momentary advantage by telling audiences what they want to hear even when we know it is nonsense. But nonsense has the ultimately fatal disadvantage of *being* nonsense. Public persons are, when they speak publicly, presumed to be public leaders. They are presumed to be—and should be—better informed on their topic than the members of their audience. Audiences rightly demand that public speakers offer the best thinking the speakers can manage, even when that thinking runs counter to the conventional wisdom. To do less is to invite, perhaps without hope of recovery, the loss of public credibility.

Only when public speakers learn how to decide whether or not to speak publicly can they respond fruitfully to legitimate speaking demands and opportunities. This will also help prevent their becoming nuisances to themselves and to others. This means we should improve our sensitivity to the personal and professional reasons for public talk and at the same time develop a healthy respect for the right of other people to be left undisturbed unless we have something worthwhile to offer them. If we do this, we will most certainly speak less than we might otherwise. But when we do speak, we will speak with greater conviction and enthusiasm, and audiences will more likely welcome our efforts.

DECIDING WHEN TO SPEAK

Once we have decided that public communication is justified, we are ready to consider *when* to speak. Here the factors to consider are heavily dependent upon widely variable topical, social, and situational elements.

Timely Topics

For example, the topic can help one decide when to speak. Recently in a Milwaukee suburb, residents learned that their village board was planning to authorize villagewide aerial spraying to control mosquitoes. The spray to be used was the same chemical that had provoked controversy during the California Medfly crisis. If opposition to the planned spraying program was to be effective, residents would have to speak up at the next meeting of the village board, for if approved at that meeting, spraying was to begin immediately. Village residents heavily attended the next board meeting, and the debate was intense with several residents speaking on both sides of the issue. When the vote was taken, the spraying program was defeated by a narrow margin. The subject matter of public speaking often carries its own time demands.

Some special events similarly contain inherent time limitations: Newly elected officers of a local company are named just prior to a large yearly meeting, and those officers are expected to make their first public speeches under their new titles at that convocation; public speakers respond to a number of formally announced deadlines that obviate the question of when to speak; an engineer appears at a formal, public bidding conference to lay out a proposal for new construction; a public relations expert prepares a presentation for an advertising campaign to meet a client's deadline; a medical researcher scrambles to complete a presentation to be delivered at the next medical convention. We are all familiar with events that impose deadlines on our opportunities for public discourse.

Social Conventions

Matters of protocol, social convention, and tradition may also direct our decision as to when to speak. It is, for example, considered politically unwise for a newly elected member of Congress to make a speech in Congress until the first legislative session is well under way; a marketing director will wisely postpone publicly announcing a new marketing campaign during the Christmas holiday season; and woe to the President of the United States who preempts prime-time television to talk about the economy on a Monday night during the football season. Sensitivity to social rituals, cherished traditions, or well-established public habits will often assist our efforts to know when to speak.

Fairness

Two other related and more subjective factors should be considered in deciding when to speak. Insofar as it is possible, speakers must manage the timing of their speaking to ensure fairness to an audience. Audiences do not like nasty surprises and proposals carefully timed late to rule out other options. The public works director of a large Eastern city was fired some years ago because he announced that a decision had been made several weeks earlier to demolish a historical landmark; he made his announcement well after a local historical restoration group had initiated a fund-raising campaign to restore the building. Audiences must be allowed time to hear and judge public pronouncements while there is still time to exercise choice. Circumventing this process by unfair manipulation of time is a strategy reserved for public rogues, charlatans, and flim-flam artists.

Speakers need to be, as far as possible, fair to themselves in deciding when to speak publicly. We generally know when we are likely to be at our best and when we are courting disaster. If, for example, you know that a speaking assignment will require two weeks of dedicated preparation effort, it is a mistake to schedule the speech within less time than that. As in all endeavors, we must learn to know our strengths, limitations, and weaknesses. And, as a rule of thumb, persons who have not yet learned to gauge their capabilities as public communicators are best advised to proceed conservatively until they become more adept at judging their limitations as public speakers.

All of this—examining the topic, the occasion, the audience, and oneself—would appear to be most useful in deciding when *not* to speak rather than when to speak. Indeed, the somewhat reluctant public speaker will find in this discussion a reason to reject virtually all public speaking opportunities. That is not the intention here. We become effective public persons as we *seek out* public speaking opportunities.

Against the Current

From time to time we will need to speak without regard to unfavorable time considerations. We may need to raise public issues after most people believe they have been decided. The Watergate issue was raised and presumably answered by the Nixon administration before the 1972 national election, but Judge John Sirica, Woodward and Bernstein of the *Washington Post*, and John Dean forced the issue before the American people. We may challenge social conventions and traditions as a means of altering them and as a means of drawing attention to urgent public matters. Certainly, fairness to ourselves and to our audiences must occasionally yield to more compelling exigencies for speaking.

Deciding whether to speak and when to speak requires judgment; the guidelines offered here are intended to assist—not determine—such judgment. The experienced public speaker will recognize occasions when it is necessary to speak even though all available evidence suggests that public speaking—especially at that moment—is inadvisable. The real value of the guidelines identified in these pages is to assist public communicators to gauge the risks of engaging in public talk at particular times.

Sometimes the risks are high but nevertheless compelling. Some years ago, a design engineer for an American automobile manufacturer discovered a major flaw in the design of a production model that was enjoying outstanding sales. His internal memoranda were dismissed as exaggerated nit-picking. To speak publicly under those circumstances was to risk destroying a career; but that engineer did speak out and ultimately forced a redesign and a major recall that saved lives.

Public speaking, to repeat a persistent theme, is inherently risky, and some risks are greater than others. The competent public communicator accepts the risks of public talk and becomes increasingly capable of precisely judging the risks of each encounter with an eye toward preparing to meet those risks.

A PREPARATION GAME

Preparing yourself for public communication now begins in earnest. Notice that "preparing yourself for public communication" implies a more complex task than "preparing a speech." Assuming that the decisions of whether to speak and when to speak have been made, I have found it useful for myself and in training others for public communication to begin by previewing the entire preparation process. Planning is apt to be more efficient and complete if we understand from the outset what has to be done from beginning to end. By previsioning the Big Picture, we can make judgments about how we should allocate our time prior to actual

114, 279

FIGURE 2.1 "The Public Presentation Game"

THE PUBLIC PRESENTATION GAME

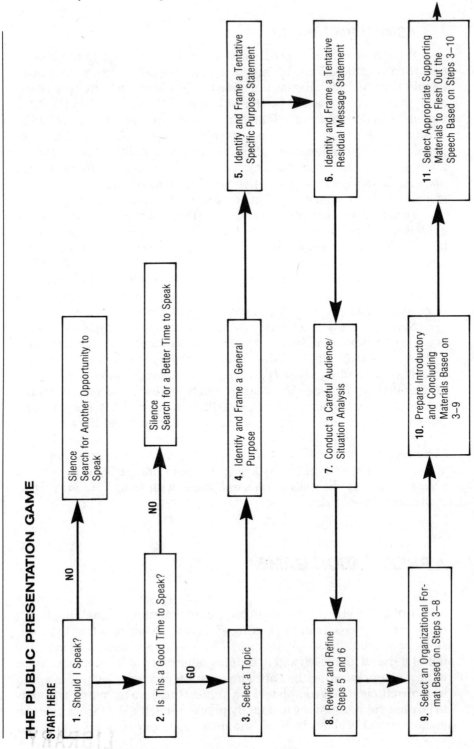

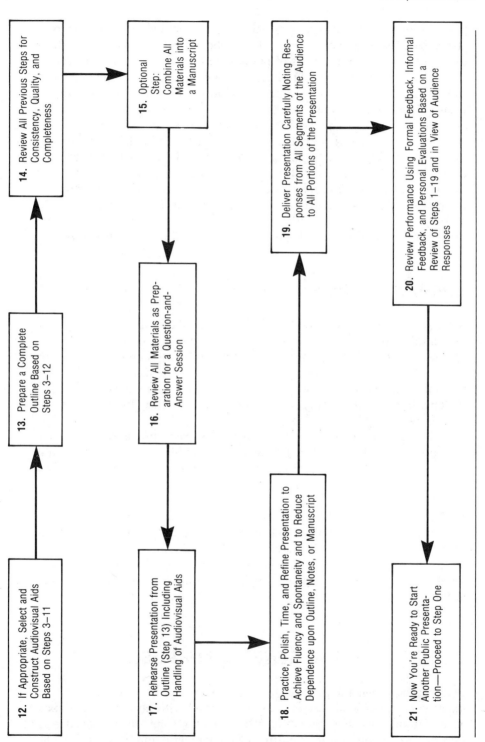

12. If Appropriate, Select and Construct Audiovisual Aids Based on Steps 3–11

13. Prepare a Complete Outline Based on Steps 3–12

14. Review All Previous Steps for Consistency, Quality, and Completeness

15. Optional Step: Combine All Materials into a Manuscript

16. Review All Materials as Preparation for a Question-and-Answer Session

17. Rehearse Presentation from Outline (Step 13) Including Handling of Audiovisual Aids

18. Practice, Polish, Time, and Refine Presentation to Achieve Fluency and Spontaneity and to Reduce Dependence upon Outline, Notes, or Manuscript

19. Deliver Presentation Carefully Noting Responses from All Segments of the Audience to All Portions of the Presentation

20. Review Performance Using Formal Feedback, Informal Feedback, and Personal Evaluations Based on a Review of Steps 1–19 and in View of Audience Responses

21. Now You're Ready to Start Another Public Presentation—Proceed to Step One

presentation and in that way ensure that our preparation will allow us to be at our best. To assist you, I offer The Public Presentation Game, an illustration of the complete process of preparing for public communication.

The remainder of this book will be devoted to explaining and illustrating each step in this intriguing game, but some observations are appropriate at this point—the rules of the game, so to speak. First, no step can be skipped without risking the failure of the entire enterprise. Second, the steps are not sequential; that is, it is within the rules to return to any previous step until Step 19 (the actual presentation) is reached. Third, the steps are not equal; some will require substantial investment of time and thought, and others should be done thoughtfully but briskly—even experimentally. This is especially true, for example, for Steps 5 and 6. Finally, as suggested by the note following Step 20, the process for the public person is continuous: once begun, the game continues indefinitely.

LOCATING TOPICS

Most professional people are not hard-pressed to identify topics for public communication. In most instances, topics will emerge from the workplace, the profession, and the community, to name merely the common sources for topics. Even though it is an important preliminary decision to be confronted by the public speaker, selection of a topic need not occupy us long. It is enough to suggest that topics are generally in greater supply than time to develop and use them.

The public person eager to test public communication skills will find plentiful subject matter to speak about publicly. As a general rule, too, we speak about the things we know and the things that stir us. Audiences search for whatever clues they can find in a public communication encounter that suggest the speaker commands his or her subject matter and is emotionally committed to it. Knowledge and enthusiasm for a subject are critical, and their lack is hard to disguise before a public group. Speak about the things you know and are eager to know even more about, and the things about which you care deeply. In most instances this will be more than adequate. In Chapter 4, I will discuss other means for identifying, testing, and choosing topics and materials to support those topics.

DETERMINING THE GENERAL PURPOSE

Determining a general purpose for public speaking is simply a matter of identifying the general response to be achieved with an anticipated audience. Public speeches generally fall into four categories; Speeches to *inform* seek to elicit understanding, awareness, and appreciation from an audience; speeches to *persuade* seek not only understanding but change in the perceptions, attitudes, and behaviors of audience members; speeches to *entertain* seek to stimulate and amuse an audience; *ceremonial addresses* seek to respond to the requirements of some significant moment or event.

Let us assume you have chosen to speak about supply-side economics. If, in the best of all possible worlds, you expect to have your audience understand and appreciate the complexities of this school of economic thought, then the general purpose is to inform. If, however, you expect to build a case for the wisdom of this economic view and gain audience support for its adoption as national economic policy, then the general purpose is persuasive.

Speeches to entertain may contain informative and persuasive elements, but material is offered more to amuse than to be taken seriously. A speech by the Washington political satirist Mark Russell may poke good-natured barbs at the vagaries of supply-side economics, but it is typically not viewed as serious economic or political commentary. Celebrity roasts, the humorous examination of personal foibles, gentle ribbing of social rituals, and tongue-in-cheek exaggeration of common situations—this is the stuff of speeches to entertain. The primary problem of the entertainment speech is to tickle without taunting and to insinuate without insulting. Speaking to entertain is, typically, the province of the polished public speaker.

Ceremonial speeches may be somber or joyous, depending on the occasion. Eulogies are part of the rich tradition of ceremonial speeches. Building and bridge dedications, anniversaries, retirements, promotions, inaugurations, high-school and college commencements, and ship christenings are but a few occasions that invite ceremonial speeches. The first responsibility of the ceremonial speaker is to understand and respond to the expectations of those who gather to mark a particular occasion.

Recently a Wisconsin political figure created a statewide controversy when he accepted an invitation to deliver a high-school commencement address for a modest fee but then used the occasion to deliver a highly partisan political statement. The disappointment and anger of students, parents, and school officials resulted in a public demand that the fee be returned. The competent ceremonial speaker yields personal objectives to the demands of the event.

IDENTIFYING A SPECIFIC PURPOSE

The general purpose identifies the overall objective of the public speech and sets limits on the discourse. In doing so, it informs the preparation of a tentative specific-purpose statement. The specific-purpose statement delimits and focuses the general purpose by tempering ambitious objectives against the realities of time limitations and likely audience predispositions. For example, I might wish to inform an audience about the economic theories that justify a politically conservative economic policy. But, given the economic naïveté of most audiences, and given time for only a twenty-minute speech rather than a seminar, I would be well-advised to focus on a more manageable topic. Perhaps I should aim for understanding of the Laffer Curve or a couple of the key tenets of George Gilder's economic views.

Types of Audiences

The specific purpose also represents the first, tentative effort to judge audience receptivity to public talk. Chapter 3 will probe in greater detail the methods for conducting a thorough analysis of specific audience relationships. But some preliminary judgments about the anticipated audience for our talk and the conditions under which we will confront that audience are necessary to the proper framing of a specific-purpose statement. Here an early but insightful classification of audience types by H. L. Hollingworth will serve us well for making this essential preliminary judgment. Hollingworth contends that public audiences fall into five major classifications, each representing particular proclivities to respond to public talk.[1]

The *pedestrian* or *casual* audience, in Hollingworth's taxonomy, is the least organized audience we can envision. Visualize the kind of audience that gathers around a booth at a state fair attracted by the vocal intensity and colorful talk of a pitchman selling electric zippers to anyone who happens to be passing. A major difficulty with such an audience is to get them to listen at all. Their gathering is accidental, their orientation toward a speaker is minimal, and their willingness to remain in place long enough to learn or accept anything is problematical. Faced with the prospect of such an audience, the public speaker would do well to frame a specific-purpose statement that reflects the difficulties of attracting and holding the attention of minimally committed listeners.

The *passive* audience is best thought of as captive listeners. They gather, typically, knowing little about what to expect from a speaker and often with widely varying interest in or hope for the encounter. Salespeople gathered for a mandatory pep talk from the new vice-president for sales, parents attending their first PTA meeting, soldiers ordered to attend a physical hygiene lecture by the camp surgeon, and college students squirming in their assigned seats to hear a guest lecture in a required course—these are passive audiences. Their presence as a group is not accidental; some common expediency draws them, but they may share little else in common than the hope that they will not have to suffer more than is necessary or longer than necessary.

The passive audience invites the speaker to win their attention, reward their presence, and galvanize them into a cohesive unit with common purpose and commitment. A specific-purpose statement drawn in anticipation of such an audience should be more ambitious than that for a pedestrian audience but with due regard to a similar need to establish and sustain interest in the discourse.

An audience that has come together for a clearly understood and shared reason is called a *selected* audience in Hollingworth's scheme. The speaker can safely assume their initial attention and interest. Members of such civic and fraternal groups as Kiwanis, Lions, and Jaycees and members of professional groups meeting in convention are examples of a selected audience. In framing a specific-purpose statement for this type of audience, the speaker should be concerned with sustaining initial interest while concentrating on establishing a good impression and moving the audience toward a predetermined goal.

Some listeners are intensively oriented toward the reason that brings them together. The party faithful who fill a hall for a preelection rally, the congregation of a church or synagogue, and physicians gathered to hear about the latest techniques for treating jogging injuries or to learn how to manage the vagaries of the money market—these are examples of a *concerted* audience. Members of such an audience typically share common values and needs; they come together with nearly identical expectations and commitments. Gaining or even sustaining the attention of such listeners is not a serious concern.

Anticipating such an audience, the speaker should construct a specific-purpose statement that focuses upon maximum exploitation of such favorable circumstances. Such audiences virtually cry out for full information, maximum persuasive effort, or some combination of both, followed by directions for action. The most frequent mistake made with concerted audiences is failing to achieve as much as their receptivities allow.

The *organized* audience, in Hollingworth's scheme, is a public communicator's dream. Like the concerted audience, members of this type of audience share common values and needs and come together eagerly with common expectations and commitments. But beyond these happy qualities, the organized audience is predisposed to accept what the speaker has to offer and move quickly toward a related course of action. Under these circumstances, the speaker must be prepared to act boldly in implementing a most ambitious purpose. To do less is to fail.

As a general approach to anticipating audience responses prior to framing a specific-purpose statement, Hollingworth's classification can be useful. Some qualifications, however, must be acknowledged. The general types of audiences Hollingworth describes are more theoretical than real, and the classifications are therefore not mutually exclusive. Some audiences we confront will be mixed audiences containing passive, selected, concerted, and organized elements. And a particular audience may be more or less concerted or organized. Then, too, circumstances may alter the general character of a particular audience. A casual audience may be so mesmerized by a street orator that their normal resistance to persuasive arguments is quickly swept away and, like an organized audience, beg to be directed toward action.

Further, Hollingworth's taxonomy is positively oriented. Each general audience type offers less resistance to the speaker and his subject than the one preceding it. This assumes that the reasons that bring people together in audiences and the values and expectations they share once they are together are similarly held by the speaker and reflected in his discourse.

The opposite, of course, may be true. A casual audience may become organized in opposition to the speaker and what he says. For example, during the Iranian hostage crisis I watched apprehensively as a group of Iranian students spoke from a platform set up on a central campus mall at the University of Wisconsin–Milwaukee. As loudspeakers blared the Iranian students' defense of the Ayatollah Khomeni and attacks on American imperialism, a crowd of students gathered, became unified in their outrage, and began shouting their opposition in unison. Only the skillful intervention of the campus police prevented an ugly incident.

Preparing a specific-purpose statement that articulates goals for public communication while acknowledging, in the first tentative way, the likely audience response is serious business. As a first judgment, it directs subsequent thinking and preparation. Consequently, while we should be open to subsequent rethinking and reframing of the specific purpose, we dare not make light of our first attempts. Careful preliminary analysis of our objectives and the likely audience receptivity—or resistance—to our message will result in a specific-purpose statement that will direct subsequent preparation in an orderly and efficient manner and preclude wasted effort.

IDENTIFYING A RESIDUAL MESSAGE

Recall if you will a public speech you have heard that you regard as both memorable and also exemplary of good public speaking. Your choice may be an inspiring sermon, a moving eulogy for a friend or loved one, a political talk, or a locker-room talk by a coach before the big game. Now, quickly, what was the single most important idea that you remember from that speech? If you can remember, try restating that thought as a complete sentence and, as closely as you can remember it, in the precise language the speaker used. Finally, working from that clearly articulated idea, try to reconstruct as much of the rest of that memorable speech as you can— again in the words used by the speaker.

Chances are good that you surprised yourself with this exercise. If you were able to recall the single most important idea and restate it in the speaker's words, you probably were then able to recall a surprising amount of that speech. In the process, you have demonstrated the nature and function of a residual message. A residual message is the central or essential idea to be found in any public speech. Like the prize in a Cracker Jack box, it is the treasure which is eagerly sought and retained after all else is removed. As the name suggests, it is the essence that remains when all else is so much vapor.

In the most widely remembered speech of his tragically short lifetime, Martin Luther King, Jr., spoke to the nation from Washington, D.C., in 1963 about his vision of this country free from racial strife. "I have a dream," he said, and spoke of his yearning to see the nation "rise up and live out the true meaning of its creed." "I have a dream," he said, and spoke of his hope that his four children would one day live in a nation where they would be judged by "the content of their character" and not the color of their skin. "I have a dream," he said, and expressed his hope that, even in the Deep South, brotherhood would replace racism. What is the residual message of this most remarkable speech? What is its essence? What single idea from it stirs our memory most vividly and helps us to recall much more than would otherwise be possible? The answer, of course, is that four-word refrain that continues to haunt the consciences of all who remember and honor this great American.

The reason for framing a tentative residual message as a part of our preliminary thinking and preparation for public speaking is, I trust, obvious. If we can early on state for ourselves clearly what we wish to say and what we want our intended audience to remember most vividly, then that idea can inform and direct all else that follows. Further, if the residual message is, as it should be, the most dramatic idea that we convey to the audience, it will serve as a catalyst to audience recall of much of our message long after we have finished speaking.

Finally, because it functions as a catalyst to more complete audience recall, the residual message becomes an important tool for measuring public communication effectiveness. Professional speech critics agree that the extent to which audiences recall and can restate the ideas used by a speaker in public discourse is an important measure of the effectiveness of the public talk. Bad speeches are forgotten for a number of reasons, but good speeches—even those that contain ideas with which we disagree— are remembered because they contain at least one idea that forces itself upon our memories.

I have suggested that, like the specific-purpose statement, the residual message should be stated tentatively as part of our early thinking and planning for public encounters. This does not suggest that the first effort to frame a residual message should be done cursorily. The residual message may change as preparation for the speech continues up to actual presentation. But those changes should be *refinements* of the essential idea of the speech, not frivolous alterations of it, because to change entirely the residual message is to change the entire thrust of the speech.

BELIEVE IN YOURSELF

Let me suggest one final aid I have found useful in preparing myself to speak and in helping others to speak. Allow me to suggest that at this stage in preparing yourself to speak, as you stand poised to continue and complete preparation for a public encounter, there is value in taking stock of what has been done and where it will lead. At this point there is value in having a quiet talk with yourself that will make the remaining preparation easier to accomplish and ensure a more confident and enthusiastic presentation.

Note that at this point the questions of whether to speak and when to speak have been answered, and several of the important questions about how to undertake preparation for speaking have similarly been addressed. Those answers are worth remembering. The means of effective public communication are now at hand; all that is needed is the determination and confidence to complete the process. Now, you need to tell yourself quietly but firmly that you can and will demonstrate your capabilities as a public communicator. Like the baseball player with the skill to play in the major leagues, you must see yourself performing successfully as a public speaker and cling tenaciously to that vision as you prepare and perform.

As a father of two small boys, I have had opportunities to watch "Mister Rogers' Neighborhood" on public television. I have been struck as perhaps you have by his ability to teach children to have confidence in their abilities. With a smile and a song he tells them that they can do many things, but they must believe they can and then act on that belief. "There's nothing to it. You got to do it," he sings, and the children learn early to respect their abilities. I am not ashamed to suggest that I find the same message personally valuable nor to suggest that it has value for you as you approach public communication. Public communication is clearly a mobile skill; you've go to *do* it to become competent and professional.

You want to succeed and you can learn how to succeed. It may be encouraging for you to know that most of the audiences you confront also want you to succeed. Recall, if you will, the last time you watched and listened to a speaker who struggled to complete a public speech. Chances are you and the rest of the audience felt uncomfortable. You empathized with the speaker and wished that somehow you could help him do a good job. And you can recall how pleased and satisfied you felt when a speaker—perhaps one that you believed would have difficulty—managed a public encounter smoothly and confidently.

I have been enthralled, as millions have, by the recent *Star Wars* movies with their intriguing mixture of adventure, philosophy, and theology. Those movies have made much of the suggestion that a Force exists around us that if recognized and accepted will permit us to do extraordinary things. Such a force exists for public speakers in the eagerness of audiences to hear well-prepared public speeches. That eagerness, that empathy, if embraced, can serve us well.

The second *Star Wars* movie introduced a fascinating character named Yoda, a gnomelike character whose role is to train selected individuals to use "The Force." In *The Empire Strikes Back*, Yoda reluctantly accepts a young man, Luke Skywalker, for training. The undertaking is difficult because Skywalker allows himself to be easily distracted from the tasks Yoda sets for him. At a critical point in the training, Yoda orders Skywalker to use his newly acquired telekinetic powers to lift his space vehicle out of a swamp. Skywalker promises to try, strains to lift the vehicle, only to lose his concentration and watch the vehicle sink back into the mire. "It can't be done; I'm not strong enough!" Skywalker protests. Frowning, the diminutive Yoda lifts his hand, concentrates, lifts the vehicle, and gently sets it on dry land. Skywalker is amazed. "I don't believe it," he shouts. A pained Yoda regards him thoughtfully and replies, "That is why you fail."

Public communication is not something you try to do half-convinced that you will fail. It is something you do because you understand what must be done and believe you can. If this chapter serves any purpose at all, it should convince you that there is nothing in the thinking and in the preparing for public communication that you cannot do if you will only commit yourself to the doing. Understand what is required, envision yourself succeeding in doing what is required, and believe that vision.

SUMMARY

I have endeavored in this chapter to lay out for you the first, critical steps in preparing to speak publicly. I have illustrated the personal, professional, audience, and situational reasons that should be reviewed in deciding whether or not to speak, and I have cautioned you—not altogether facetiously—to avoid being a nuisance as a public speaker. I have asked you to become sensitive to the topical, social, and situational factors that allow you to judge the appropriate time to speak. I have urged you to be fair to your anticipated audience and to yourself in judging when to speak. I have encouraged you to seek opportunities to speak publicly even if that means occasionally challenging what may appear to be formidable justifications for not speaking at a particular time or for not speaking at all.

Assuming justification for speaking at some identifiable time, I have urged an orientation toward preparing yourself for public communication rather than merely preparing a speech. I have argued the value of previsioning the complete planning process as a means of ensuring systematic and efficient planning for public discourse; I have asked you to consider The Public Presentation Game as a means of mapping a thorough strategy for achieving public speaking effectiveness. I have suggested ways of identifying topics for public speaking and reviewed the general purposes for public discourse. I have argued that tentative specific-purpose statements should delimit and focus the general purpose through recognition of the constraints imposed by time limitations and general audience receptivities. I have discussed the nature and values of a carefully drawn residual message statement as a guide for all subsequent preparation. And finally, I have urged the importance of *believing it can be done.*

Note

1. This section has profited from a review of Hollingworth, H. L., *The Psychology of the Audience* (New York: American Book Company, 1935), 19–32, as well as discussions of Hollingworth's classifications found in Ewbank, H. L., and Auer, J. J., *Discussion and Debate* (New York: F. S. Crofts, 1945), 222–24; and Brooks, W. D., *Public Speaking* (Reading, Mass.: Benjamin/Cummings, 1980), 155–57.

CHAPTER 3

You Gotta Know the Territory: Analyzing Public Communication Situations

The opening number from Meredith Willson's *The Music Man*[1] features a musical argument among a group of salesmen on a train early in this century. As the train moves along they debate the merits of cash sales for buttonhooks, demijohns, hogsheads, and noggins, and they discuss the unorthodox selling techniques of a certain Mr. Harold Hill. Despite their disagreements, the salesmen are agreed that to be successful in selling anything "You Gotta Know the Territory."

SITUATIONAL ANALYSIS

As indicated earlier, public communication is adapted to conditions: we as speakers achieve our purposes through listeners with messages uniquely tailored to them and to the circumstances and settings in which we meet those listeners. While this may sound stuffy and complex, it is familiar—perhaps obvious. We would not, for example, attempt to sell a new computer system to a client who has recently purchased and installed a competitive system. We would, perhaps, find that a good time to sell software that is compatible with and will improve the efficiency and utility of the new system.

In communicative activity we intuitively search for the right audience, the most favorable time and circumstance, and the most appropriate message. We wait for the boss to be in the right mood to ask for a raise. We avoid making sales calls the day before major holidays, and we look for just the right moment to propose marriage, announce a promotion, or initiate a sales campaign. In our daily private and public activities we are sensitive to the need to adapt messages to fit particular people in particular circumstances. Adaptation, however, presumes good information and careful analysis of that information. This chapter addresses these concerns.

Knowing the territory for public communication is a matter of examining five elements and the relationships among those elements, found in all public speaking encounters. We readily understand the need to gather and analyze information about the people who will likely be the targets of our public messages. Indeed, most public speaking textbooks and manuals contain an obligatory chapter on "audience analysis." But audiences do not materialize in a vacuum. How members of an audience respond to a public message is determined not only by their commonalities as people but also by their unique and defining characteristics as individuals who respond to a particular message from a particular speaker under particular circumstances and in a specified location.

The term *audience analysis* is inadequate to our needs. To know the territory for public communication, we must undertake a complex analysis of the speaking situation; we must examine *speaker, audience, context, setting,* and *message* and the relationships among these elements during a public speaking encounter.

Further, knowing the territory for public communication is a matter of three levels of analysis—each level requiring something different from us. First, we must attempt to prevision the speaking situation as part of our preparation. Second, since we cannot expect to know all we may need to know about a speaking encounter until it takes place, we must become adept at reading and responding to speaking situations as they are taking place. We will refer to this level of analysis as *process* or ongoing analysis. Finally, if we are to make the most of each public communication experience, we must learn to understand and evaluate each experience. This level of analysis we'll call *postanalysis.*

If this is beginning to sound like the rules for three-dimensional chess or the latest economic plan for lowering interest rates and whipping inflation, I hope you'll bear with me for a moment. Let's return to Harold Hill chugging his way into a small Iowa town looking for people "as green as their money" so that he can sell band instruments and uniforms and false promises of musical training. He looks at himself—a good place for any public speaker to begin analysis prior to public speaking. As just plain Harold Hill, salesman, he's not very impressive. But, given his purpose, being impressive as a musical impresario will be essential to his success. Being a con artist, he has a quick—if dangerous—remedy for that problem; he becomes "Professor" Harold Hill, a colleague of such then-prominent musicians as Pat Conway, W. C. Handy, and the renowned John Philip Sousa.

When he arrives in town, he begins gathering information about his targeted audience, the setting, and the salient circumstances—anything that will help him achieve his purpose through a masterfully adapted message. He watches, notes, questions, and listens to the River City folk. What commonalities bind them? What common likes and dislikes, what hopes, fears, and prejudices are suggested by their talk, behavior, and trappings? What differences divide them? What egocentric views and behaviors are tolerated if not encouraged? What behaviors or characteristics receive social censure? He attempts to learn their collective and personal histories so that he has a clearer picture of present circumstances. His is a thorough prior analysis of the "territory" or the situation in which he expects to get people to do what he wants them to do, but for their own reasons.

As a result of his preliminary observations and analyses, Professor Hill reaches an important conclusion. He decides that a series of messages will be necessary to achieve his goals. First, he will have to attract and focus attention on a problem that the townspeople will readily recognize and see as urgent (in this case the pool hall). Then, after they are convinced there is "trouble in River City," he can begin to sell the idea of a boys' band to keep the River City youths "moral after school."

Necessarily, then, he will have to be alert to the reactions of his listeners while he speaks. He prepares himself to monitor closely the reactions of townspeople, parents, town officials, and a skeptical town librarian named Marian. Their reactions to his argument will be important to his message strategies in subsequent and related public performances. Clearly, too, he will have to evaluate his performance at its completion, using whatever data he can gather. In addition to a careful personal review of his speaking, he will check the talk and behavior of the townspeople who will hear his first performance. What do they have to say among themselves and to others who were not present for his first, masterfully adapted pitch? Postanalysis then will become prior preparation for subsequent public speeches.

The last thing I would suggest is that you emulate the mind set and message strategies of a professional con artist like Harold Hill. But this example may serve to make the complexities of prior, process, and postsituational analysis less formidable. For the remainer of this chapter I will examine step-by-step the methods and means for conducting a thorough situational analysis. I will suggest ways of adapting message strategies to fit people in particular circumstances and settings. Next, I will suggest how you can make the most of ongoing or process analysis. Finally, I will offer some straightforward procedures for conducting a postanalysis of the speaking encounter. We need not be as impishly deceitful as Professor Harold Hill to become as masterfully adaptive as he was depicted to be in Meredith Willson's delightful musical production.

Let me suggest at the outset that situational analysis is best viewed as detective work. We must become public communication sleuths. Clues, we will see, lie all around us; some are missed because they are obvious, and others are artfully concealed from us. As detectives we have two major objectives. First, we must be careful not to miss anything. Our research must be exhaustive; better to overdo than risk missing the one piece of data, the one clue that solves the mystery and promotes the success of our public communication efforts. Then we need the savvy to separate the telling information from the trivial. No amount of information will be adequate if we cannot judge its saliency to the public communication situation at hand, whereas even very little information will serve us well if it is the right kind of information.

PRIOR ANALYSIS

The first and major portion of this chapter will examine the processes of prior situational analysis. Clearly, prior analysis is a matter of previsioning the anticipated speaking encounter. Some years ago, Time-Life Films produced an instructional film that featured Robert Morse, star of the movie *How to Succeed in Business Without Really Trying.*[2] Morse portrays a genie in a three-piece suit who assists a harried and confused businessman to prepare for an important public presentation. Over and over he invites his student to visualize himself in the anticipated situation so that the features of that situation will become clearer and so that his preparation will have focus. There is, of course, nothing magical or unusual in such previsioning; we do it all the time for all sorts of reasons. If you're planning to play golf on the weekend, you can readily envision yourself teeing up on the first hole. You see yourself selecting the proper club, testing the wind, and swinging through at the ball. In your mind you see amazing detail: the golf course, your companions; you can practically feel the heat and smell the grass. Perceptual psychologists call this prevision a reification.

A *reification* of a public speaking encounter is simply the vision we construct in our heads in anticipation of a public speaking situation. It is necessarily subjective and inferential. Reifications help us predict and prepare for anticipated events. Importantly, we respond in the actual situations as our reifications have prepared us to respond. If, for example, we prevision ourselves addressing a highly receptive, organized audience, we will likely respond in the actual situation with message strategies which assume attention and interest and move quickly toward reinforcement and a call to action. Whether these strategies are appropriate and consequently successful is dependent upon the degree of similarity between our self-constructed mental image of the anticipated situation and the realities of the situation as it unfolds. The trick, of course, is to make our reifications as reliably representative and predictive of actual events as we can manage. Prior situational analysis is, then, a matter of attempting to be as objective as we can in making essentially subjective and probabilistic judgments about anticipated public speaking encounters. And since we do not have a crystal ball or a kindly genie to guide us, we will have to rely upon systematic techniques that will direct our efforts and lead to probable but never guaranteed success in anticipating and responding to public communication situations.

The Speaker

Prior situational analysis begins with a careful look at ourselves as potential public speakers. What are our qualifications for speaking on the subject we have chosen or been driven to accept? How emotionally involved are we with the subject matter? To what extent has our public behavior reflected concern and involvement with the subject matter of the anticipated speech? In general, how credible on this subject matter are we? In other words, how widespread is our reputation for expertise on this subject matter? These questions do not exhaust the possibilities for self-examination, but they provide a start. Later, as we examine the relationships among speaker, audience, message, circumstances, and setting, other questions will receive attention. For now, let's examine this set of questions to ensure understanding of what is being asked. A question well understood is one that practically answers itself.

Qualification for speaking on a subject is a matter of knowledge and experience. The combination here is important. Let me illustrate. Following World War II hundreds of books appeared in print by soldiers and sailors who were anxious to explain in print their combat experiences and their perspectives on that global conflict. As personal stories and as descriptions of some part of events in some specific area of one of several theaters of war, many of these stories were interesting and of certain historical value. But as books about World War II they were clearly inadequate, since most had only limited personal perspectives on complex events that in some way touched the lives of every person on the planet. Knowledge of World War II would require understanding of many personal perspectives, the strategies, tactics, and events occuring simultaneously around the globe, and the way those events were interrelated. As an amateur historian of that period, I find most valuable books like William Manchester's *Goodbye Darkness*, which begins with personal experience and perspective but moves to a broader examination of Allied actions in the Pacific. Manchester saw action on the beaches of Tarawa, but he did not fight on Peleliu. His extensive postwar research, however, gives an authoritative ring to his characterization of the bloody landings at Peleliu as "Tarawa without a seawall."[3]

As you ask yourself about your qualifications on your subject matter, envision an audience that expects and deserves as much of the complete picture as you can provide. Realize, too, that knowledge of the subject matter is often not enough. You and I would not trust our lives to an airline pilot who has earned a perfect score on a written test about flying but has never actually flown, or to an air traffic controller who has completed all but hands-on course work. Audiences are most responsive to speakers who are fully informed on their subject matter and have extensive and related experiences.

How can you and I anticipate the ways an audience will test the extent of our qualifications for speaking? Among the most obvious test is the extent to which a speaker speaks the language of the subject matter. For example, I would expect an engineer specializing in the design of diesel engines for automobiles to know and speak easily about Roosa pumps, cetane ratings, and diesel oil qualification tests.

A further test of qualifications for speaking is often found in our struggle to fit what we know into a single speech. As a general rule our qualifications are sufficient when we know far more than we can manage in a single speech, when we have materials enough for several speeches exploring various facets of the topic, and when we feel confident that we can answer virtually any question the anticipated audience can ask on the topic. Finally, we are likely to meet the audience's test for sufficient qualifications on the subject matter when we know enough to recognize the limitations of our knowledge and experience on the subject matter. A favorite and appropriate question from doctoral committees examining candidates for a Ph.D. is "What is it that you do not know about the area of your most intensive research?" If we are thoroughly qualified in a particular area or subject matter we are typically keenly aware of what we do not know and still have to learn.

Assuming that we believe ourselves to be qualified to speak on a subject, we can turn to the question of personal involvement. Usually, if our knowledge and experience in an area are extensive, we are involved with the subject matter; we find it difficult to become expert on matters that do not interest and attract us—although there are exceptions. What we are looking for here is that spark, that eagerness, that sense of conviction and urgency that makes it difficult for us to tolerate the thought of not speaking publicly. When you feel you have something important to offer an audience, when you are convinced that you are as well prepared as anyone else to speak, and when you yearn for an opportunity to do so, then you have answered the question about personal involvement with the topic.

The question, of course, is critical to your success as a public communicator. Audience members readily recognize personal involvement— or the lack of it—in a speaker. We have no right to expect audience members to respond with any more interest, concern, conviction, and enthusiasm than we display when speaking before them. Indeed, audiences will excuse all sorts of errors in speakers who clearly believe personally in what they say; but the same audiences will not forgive even experienced, polished speakers who signal personal detachment from a message.

Personal involvement is often best indicated by previous public behavior, including previous public speaking. Ralph Nader, for example, may be accused of many things, but he is not likely to be accused even by his severest critics of being uncommitted or personal uninvolved in his public advocacy of strong consumerism. Before his resignation, James Watt, Secretary of the Interior in the Reagan administration, was severely criticized by environmental groups for his positions on conservation and resource development, but his critics respected his near-religious, public advocacy of his points of view on such matters. Audiences are surprisingly sensitive to previous public statements and behavior which bespeak personal involvement and conviction.

An interesting but rare exception to this general rule of consistent public behavior is evident in the case of what I will call "public repentants." Former presidential aide Charles Colson is an example. For many years Colson typified in his public statements and behavior a cynical, no-holds-barred approach to national politics. Then, during the late stages of the Watergate investigations, he had a change of heart. He was convicted of several crimes and served out his sentence in federal prison as a model prisoner. In public statements before and after his incarceration he spoke of his personal religious reawakening. Now, he travels about the country publicly acknowledging his past errors and urging businesspeople, political officials, and others to rededicate themselves as he has to high standards of ethical behavior.

Other examples of public repentants are familiar. Ex-convicts are often compelling public speakers on topics as the prevention of thefts and assaults and the need for prison reform. Former Communists speak with strong credibility on the virtues of a free enterprise system of government, and former government employees are effective public critics of waste in military and social programs. Typically, audiences demand that public repentants acknowledge their own complicity in what they now condemn and demonstrate their willingness to pay for past mistakes. Charles Colson is credible because he did plead guilty and went to jail, and government employees who forfeited their jobs for an uncertain future are more credible than those who argue for reinstatement to the public payroll. Self-serving or sour-grapes criticism is unimpressive. The credible repentant is someone who erred, publicly acknowledges past errors, and has in some tangible way suffered as a result of those errors. Such cases are rare but when authentic satisfy the demand of audiences that a speaker speak from strong personal involvement and commitment to the subject matter of the public talk.

For the moment, this concludes our efforts to prevision and analyze the role speakers must play in an anticipated public speaking encounter. Notice two things about this discussion: First, while it focused on one of the five elements to be considered, it necessarily dealt with relationships among all the elements. The speaker is considered in relationship to anticipated subject matter, audience, context, and setting. Subsequent analysis of these remaining factors and their interrelationships will reveal still more questions about what will be demanded from or permitted to speakers in the anticipated speaking encounter. Second, most of the questions raised focused on the relationship of the speaker to the specific audience, and definitive answers to these questions must await a more systematic examination of the nature and propensities of the expected or targeted audience. For this reason our focus next turns to the audience and the relationship of the audience to speaker, context, setting, and message.

Given the importance of knowing the audience in our efforts to analyze and adapt message strategies, you may wonder why I chose to focus on the speaker first. In fact, there is no necessary reason for doing so. The need is for systematic analysis, which ensures thorough coverage of all salient questions, and that analysis may begin anywhere. Even a cursory examination of our role as speaker may be beneficial in reinforcing or revising earlier judgments about whether to speak or when to speak. If, for example, we discover that we are not sufficiently qualified to speak on the subject matter or if we are not likely to be seen as sufficiently committed to the topic by a particular audience, we may wish to postpone or redirect our preparation for public speaking. Further efforts at prior situational analysis would be obviated by such a decision. Focusing first on the speaker may save ourselves time and effort.

Further, my preference for a first focus on the speaker is intended as a reminder that the motivations for public communication are mostly personal. The hazard in conducting a situational analysis prior to speaking is that we may lose track of what brought us to speaking in the first place as we grapple with specific questions of how to adapt ourselves and our messages to a particular audience under particular circumstances and in a particular setting. That hazard must be resisted if our public communication efforts are to be more than exercises in saying only what audiences want to hear. Prior situational analysis is not a search for the lowest common denominator; it is, rather, a search for the most effective means for accomplishing our goals in public encounters.

The Audience

Knowing the territory for public communication means knowing and adapting to the anticipated audience. But knowing the audience for a public encounter requires us to think about anticipated listeners as individuals with differences as well as commonalities. As Theodore Clevenger, Jr., has noted, the noun *audience* encourages the perception of listeners as part of a collective, a group that responds in a uniform way. That perception must be qualified to reflect the important individual differences found in any collection of people. Clevenger writes:

> Sometimes, to be sure, the members of an audience will react so similarly that they can, for all practical purposes, be regarded as a faceless flock or herd of essentially identical persons who move together as a coherent whole; but this is a very special case. Usually, we must be prepared to account for diversity in both audience make-up and audience response.[4]

As we prevision the anticipated listeners for public communication, we confront the necessity of accounting for individual differences as well as commonalities. Adaptation then becomes a matter of selecting strategies which allow us to be effective with either the greatest number of listeners or with some smaller number of listeners whose responses are critical to the achievement of our purposes in public speaking.

To illustrate, let's return to Harold Hill and his efforts to separate the citizens of River City, Iowa, from their money. It is evident that many of the people who heard Hill speak were of little or no value to him in his efforts to sell band instruments and uniforms. Unmarried individuals, for example, could hardly be expected to be directly concerned about the moral welfare of River City boys, except perhaps as a matter of altruistic civic concern. Visitors to River City could well have been part of the audience when Hill exhorted them to recall such Americanisms as Plymouth Rock, the Golden Rule, and the Maine, but these visitors, too, were not part of Hill's targeted audience.

In public communication encounters there are likely to be a number of people who are present to hear the speaker's message, but because of their disinterest in the topic cannot be considered part of the speaker's intended audience. This is especially true of public speaking situations involving the electronic or print media. At best, such listeners may serve to pass on the speaker's message to other people who may have a more direct concern with the message. At worst, such listeners may complicate the speaker's task because they lack the necessary background to understand the nature and importance of the speaker's message, because they represent potential sources of message distortion, or because their value systems are sufficiently different from the value systems of the intended audience to produce active opposition to the speaker's message. Imagine, for example, the consequences if a salesman for pool tables had been among those who heard Harold Hill's indictment of the River City pool hall. Nothing in Hill's message anticipated such a complication.

Unintended listeners may complicate our efforts to adapt messages to specified listeners. Others who hear our message may be interested for different reasons. For example, Harold Hill's audience consisted of a number of River City parents whose sons were potential habitués of the town pool hall. To these people, Hill spoke most directly and effectively. In the same audience, however, were other parents, town officials, and citizens who were interested, not because they were parents or guardians of boys at an impressionable age, but rather because they saw the issue as one of major social and civic concern. Professor Hill's message strategies clearly anticipated such concerns and were adapted to them. And Hill's audience included Marian, the town librarian, who, as a piano teacher and the town's unofficial arbiter of culture, did not need to be convinced of the value of a boys' band. Her concern was directed toward Hill's credentials as a musical impresario. Hill's grandiose efforts to establish this credibility were less than convincing for Marian; she recognized a flimflam in what she saw and heard. Hill quickly recognized the special challenge posed by Marian and developed a series of personal messages to win her.

Even this cursory review of a hypothetical audience situation illustrates several important considerations for examining audiences in anticipation of public communication. First, some who hear our public message will be disinterested in it or will view it as unrelated to their immediate needs and concerns. Others who hear our message may see it as related to their needs and concerns, but their views will differ sharply from those listeners we consider to be the targets of our message. Finally, our intended listeners may differ among themselves in their motivations for attending to and accepting our message. The audience is, in fact, a *number* of audiences which must be differentiated so that specific adaptations can be incorporated into our message. This process of moving from an undifferentiated audience to the *speaker's* audience is illustrated in Figure 3.1.

At the beginning, all potential listeners are part of the audience (I). Then, as specific information is obtained about individuals and groupings of individuals in the audience, differentiations based upon the potential salience of the message and likely listener responses can be made (II). Finally, those auditors who will most likely see the speaker's message as relevant to some concerns they have are identified and differentiated from those for whom the message is not intended (III). The speaker's audience (IV) will be composed of listeners who share some common values but also bring to the encounter specific concerns which differ but must nevertheless be accommodated within the message strategies devised by the speaker. Adaptation is then a matter of excluding some listeners and attempting to accommodate diverse and unevenly overlapping concerns and needs among others we regard as important in achieving our public

FIGURE 3.1 The Speaker's Audience

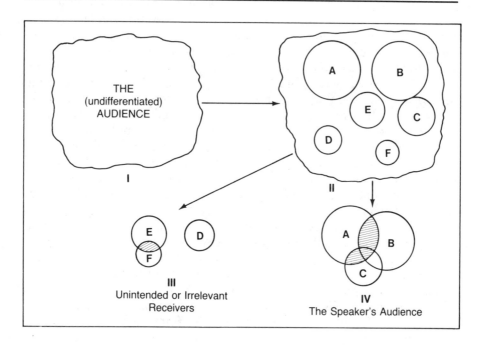

communication purposes. This task of differentiated adaptation is rightly viewed as a test of the speaker's artistry.

Previsioning the audience for public communication begins, then, by identifying the general features of the anticipated listeners. The speaker examines cultural and sociological data—data which suggest some of the gross similarities and differences existing among the anticipated listeners. In most instances, the question of major cultural differences or similarities is quickly resolved.

Most public speeches by professional people in this country will be directed to listeners who share a common cultural heritage. Occasionally, however, "American" audiences include visitors from other countries, newly arrived immigrants, and first-generation American citizens with different cultural heritages. Public speakers need to be alert to cultural differences that may exist among potential listeners. Adaptations in the content, language, and delivery of the message may be necessitated because of evident cultural diversity; perhaps the most appropriate measure to take in preparing to speak to a culturally diverse audience is prespeech conferences with representatives of the cultural groups or individuals who will be present.

Sociological data include demographics, reference groups, and information about prevailing attitude and value systems. Like cultural data, sociological data will assist our efforts to identify the similarities and differences among anticipated listeners. With further analysis, this information can suggest how particular groupings of listeners are likely to respond to the speaker's message. Demographic data include information about ages, sexes, races, educational levels, occupations, socioeconomic levels, political affiliations, religious affiliations, geographic backgrounds, and information channels to which members of the anticipated audience expose themselves. Other kinds of demographic data may be familiar to you. The purpose here is not to account for all the available demographic data, but rather to identify the most common kinds of demographic information which can assist our efforts to identify groupings of potential listeners and the degree of homogeneity within groupings of listeners.

The salience of any particular piece of demographic data must be judged by reference to the purpose and content of the speaker's message. Given the almost inexhaustible supply of available demographic data, I recommend seeking only those aspects likely to influence listeners' responses to your purpose and message.

For example, let's assume that an engineer is planning a presentation for a group of professional engineers concerning new techniques for removing chemical pollutants from the soil and water. There is no particular value in this instance to gathering information about the ages, races, sexes, occupations, religious affiliations, or political affiliations of these listeners. The topic and the fact that only professional engineers will be present make information about these demographic factors irrelevant.

Other demographic data, however, may be relevant. The educational levels of the engineers present may be important. If, for example, most of those present hold advanced degrees in chemical engineering, complex information may be presented in a short period of time. If most of the engineers present subscribe to a variety of professional chemical engineering journals and newsletters in which articles have appeared treating related aspects of chemical pollution treatment, then less time need be devoted to what otherwise would be necessary background information. As good detectives, we must consider all potentially relevant sources, and demographic data can tell us much that we need to know. On the other hand, there is little value in gathering data irrelevant to the purpose and content of our message and to our efforts to adapt to the response potentialities of particular listeners.

Another form of sociological data which can help us identify salient clusters of anticipated listeners is the concept of the reference group. A reference group is simply any group whose perspective a person shares.[5] Reference groups include the political, social, religious, and other groups to which an individual actually belongs and the groups to which the individual aspires. For example, I may be a member of a local conservation club and aspire to membership in the national Sierra Club. Listeners' reference groups provide us with important information about attitudes, values, and behavioral norms which link or separate potential listeners.

Individual listeners, of course, belong or aspire to many reference groups, and it is the *pattern* of reference groups which interests us most. A listener may be a Republican, a Catholic, and a member of the American Civil Liberties Union. In addition, he or she may agree with the objectives of the Urban League and the League of Women Voters. A listener's reference groups provide valuable information about the values and attitudes that that listener and similar others are likely to hold toward the speaker's topic. Knowledge about the reference groups represented in a particular audience will allow us to cluster groups of listeners on the basis of similarities and differences in their orientations toward the topic and our purpose in discussing the topic.

The concept of the reference group may assist our efforts to differentiate among members of a potential audience in another less direct way. Just as we belong or aspire to some groups, we view other groups negatively. Such groups are often used to assist us to know what we stand against as well as to clarify what we stand for. For example, an individual who is a Democrat, a Protestant, a member of the AFL-CIO, and a supporter of the National Organization for Women, would likely view Jerry Falwell and the Moral Majority negatively. If Jerry Falwell endorses a political candidate on behalf of the Moral Majority, that endorsement alone will provoke opposition to the candidate. Indeed, like positive reference groups, negative reference groups provide an efficient if not objective means of making judgments on a variety of issues. If, as public speakers interested in analyzing the likely responses of anticipated listeners to our purposes and subject matter, we can identify salient reference groups and negative reference groups then we can more accurately identify the differences in attitudes, beliefs, and values which characterize various segments of listeners in the anticipated audience.

People share attitudes and values with other people. Individuals attempt to align their own attitudes and values with those other individuals they respect and admire. Very often, overt behaviors, mannerisms, and even dress suggest the prevailing attitudes and values among a particular group of people. The "IBM suit" expresses not only a style of business dress but also a spectrum of attitudes and values—a mind set which characterizes those who choose to work for IBM. The skillful public communicator looks for such commonalities among potential listeners. Often several rather distinct clusters of individuals can be identified within the potential audience.

As a university teacher, I enjoy sizing up each class at the beginning of each semester. Predictably, in a class of forty students there will be several distinct groupings of students. The largest group, but not necessarily the majority of the class, is composed of men and women between the ages of 18 and 25. They are full-time students enamored of university life. They wear the standard university student "uniform," which includes faded jeans, hiking boots or jogging shoes, sport shirts or blouses, and the ubiquitous hiking knapsack. They are usually serious students with high value for practical learning; they will tolerate theory but applaud illustrations of direct, career applications of knowledge. A smaller group of students look like illustrations from the *Preppie Handbook*. They are, typically, young and bright students more interested in theory than application; they are full-time students who do not hold part-time jobs, and they are more likely to be majors in liberal arts programs. Another small group of students appear to be campus radicals with shorter hair. They are more interested in campus politics and social causes. As students they are quixotic and difficult to predict; when interested they are consummate students, but they easily and inexplicably become indifferent. Increasingly, classes on this urban campus contain some number of older students, men and women who are completing studies begun years earlier before career and family concerns interrupted. These students are serious, accepting of theoretical as well as applied knowledge, and bemused but not often irritated by the other approaches to education evinced by their classmates.

The audiences which professional people confront will similarly contain a number of subgroupings, each representing particular attitudes, values, behaviors, biases, and styles. By focusing upon demographic features, membership- and reference-group affiliations, and commonalities and differences in attitudes and values, the professional communicator discovers the opportunities and impediments to skillful message adaptations. Knowing the territory includes knowing how an audience is composed of subgroups likely to respond differently to the speaker and the speaker's message.

Harold Hill, for all his shortcomings as an ethical person, was a keen judge of character. He realized, as must all professional speakers, that it is necessary to identify key individuals within an audience who will influence the outcome of the public encounter. Within every audience are individuals who wield disproportionate influence and who require special attention. For example, Hill quickly identified the wife of the mayor of River City, four city council members, and the librarian, Marian, as persons who would strongly influence the outcome of his efforts to sell a complete boys' band. He made it his business to discover what he could do about each of these individuals.

Focusing on individual members of the total audience is a familiar and important requirement for conducting a thorough audience analysis prior to speaking. As a professional communication consultant I have assisted in the preparation of many professional presentations. One of my notable failures occurred in assisting an advertising agency prepare a presentation before a seven-person board of directors of a retail organization. The contract, if won, would have been worth more than $3,000,000. Preparation was thorough. Information on the organization and its history in the region was collected. Previous advertising efforts were examined. The board of directors, viewed as a group, was analyzed, based upon interviews and readily available information. The personal habits, preferences, and proclivities of the individual board members were examined. A masterful presentation well-adapted to the board was prepared and presented. It did not win the contract. Why? Because our analysis of a key member of the board was seriously flawed. His niece had been used for some years as the spokesperson for the company in their radio and television ads. We had recommended an advertising campaign which eliminated the niece, without realizing there was a family relationship involved. Failure to understand and adapt to key members of the audience can be hazardous.

Prior analysis of the anticipated audience is a process of moving from general similarities to the characteristics of subgroups within the audience and to individual differences. Data are collected in many ways: interviews, public records, discussions with mutual acquaintances, observations.

A successful salesman I know describes his technique for sizing up a company and its key personnel in making a first visit to their place of business. He notices the parking lot as he drives in. Is it paved in concrete or asphalt? Concrete usually indicates a more prosperous company. Is the lot well maintained and free of debris? Is there a guard on duty to direct visitors? Are guest slots close to the entrance? These details suggest a proud image and a desire to impress visitors.

As he enters the building the salesman takes note of landscaping, decor, and furnishings. Do these suggest a no-nonsense, practical orientation, a flair for creativity and innovation, or a subdued, conservative elegance? What kind of office equipment is evident? The presence of word processors and sophisticated telephone/intercom systems suggest a desire for high efficiency and a progressive image as well as reflecting the prosperity of the firm. Manual typewriters, bulky file systems, and older telephone equipment convey a different image. How is the receptionist dressed and groomed? Is the waiting area well appointed and comfortable? What kinds of magazines, trade journals, and newspapers, if any, are available in the waiting area? These often suggest important attitudes and values.

When the contact person becomes available, the salesman focuses on that person's dress, mannerisms, and office. These often provide important clues about the person. A handshake, the position of the person while conducting the interview—seated behind a desk or in a chair close to the salesman—and even the quantity of material on the office desk and tables provide additional clues about the company and the contact person. All of these observation precede the first meaningful exchange of words! Other key observations, of course, follow during the initial interview. That salesman is, not surprisingly, very successful. Effective public communicators need to develop, as this salesman has, increasingly sensitive antennae for gathering information about people.

The Context

Public communication encounters do not occur in a vacuum. Each encounter has a particular history and carries particular contextual meaning. The context shapes and constrains the discourse which can and does occur. A simple example will illustrate the point here.

In early March 1982, Wisconsin Governor Lee Dreyfus delivered his budget message before the legislature. Wisconsin was at the time experiencing a serious economic recession: Unemployment exceeded the national average, a number of major industrial plants had laid off thousands of employees, and the state was projecting a sizable budget deficit. In the weeks preceding the budget message the governor had proposed major budget cuts for all state agencies and services, and increases in corporate taxes as well as the state sales tax. When the governor appeared before the legislature, his message was predictable. He called for austerity in spending and a program of taxes to reduce the anticipated state budget deficit. His message was consistent with his previous public statements, with the events which preceded and influenced his comments, and with audience expectations. To prevision the context of a public speech is to acknowledge and adapt to those events past and present which impinge directly or indirectly upon the subject matter of the talk.

Harold Hill took pains to discover the history and flavor of life in River City, Iowa, and he seized upon the recent appearance of a pool hall in that conservative community to make his case. President Ronald Reagan, in asking for unprecedented peace-time military spending in this country, pointed to historical and continuing evidence of Soviet aggression around the world, particularly in Poland and Afghanistan, as well as evidence of a massive buildup of Russian offensive weapon systems.

The point is obvious. Effective public communication must be timely and specifically adapted to the milieu in which it takes place. Public communicators must understand that audience members attribute particular meanings to messages based upon the contexts in which those messages occur. The speaker attempts to determine how potential listeners will judge the message against their understandings of the context in which the message is presented.

The Setting

Experienced public speakers typically have a horror story or two to tell of misjudgments about the setting of a past speaking encounter. A business acquaintance of mine, for example, once prepared an impressive presentation using charts and slides for a small industrial company. He had analyzed the company's needs and preferences carefully and adapted his presentation accordingly. His charts and slides were specifically tailored to the firm. He had practiced and polished his presentation with particular attention to the smooth incorporation of the critical visual aids.

He arrived at the company a few minutes before his scheduled presentation and was taken to the room where it would take place. He was shocked. The room, a former mailroom, was long, narrow, sparsely furnished with folding chairs, and flooded by sunlight from two large, undraped windows. In addition, fluorescent lights which turned on from a single switch illuminated every corner of the room. No viewing screen was available and the walls were cinderblocks painted industrial green. The businessman had neglected to bring either a viewing screen or an easel to hold his charts. His only option was to muddle through the presentation without the slides. He attempted to hold up his charts and carry them about the room so the audience members could see them. The audience was patient but not impressed. Later he received a short, formal note thanking him for his presentation, and indicating that the contract had been awarded to a competitor.

Experienced professional communicators learn quickly to discover as much as possible about the setting before speaking. Besides discovering aspects of the setting which can cause trouble, the speaker may note particular features which may affect audience receptivities. Comfortable chairs scattered throughout the room may suggest the value of a less formal presentation, during which the speaker moves among the audience members. The presence of important symbols like the flag, religious trappings, and portraits of honored individuals provide the speaker with opportunities to demonstrate agreement with cherished audience values and beliefs. Often, seating and platform arrangements can be altered to fit the speaker's needs. Since the setting will have impact upon the speaker and the audience, the professional communicator will devote time before speaking to a careful analysis of its potentialities and hazards. At minimum, prior analysis of the setting is justified by a healthy respect for Murphy's Law: "If anything can possibly go wrong, it will."

FIGURE 3.2   Elements of Prior Analysis

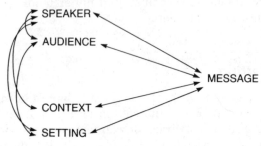

The Message

Harold Hill chugged into River City with a particular purpose in mind and a general idea of what his pitch, or message, would include. But he realized, as we must, that the message must be adapted to the particular speaking situation he confronted. While the purpose and the fundamental message remained what it was when he stepped off the train, its form was shaped by the constraints and potentialities which the speaking situation presented. By examining the relationships among speaker, audience, context, and setting, Harold Hill discovered the means for adapting the message to a particular audience, at a particular time, and in a particular setting. In those adaptations lay the basis for Hill's success. Effective public communicators must emulate Harold Hill's method if not his morals. We will look closely at message construction in the next chapter.

PROCESS ANALYSIS

Prior situational analysis is preparation for ongoing or process analysis. The speaking encounter is the occasion for directly verifying the accuracy of our efforts to prevision and adapt to particular speaking situations. It is this and more. A successful public speaker learns to look for the unexpected, to note deviations from expected responses both obvious and subtle. Process analysis demands that we observe accurately and completely what happens as we speak.

This is easier said than done. The trouble is that we tend to see what we have prepared ourselves to see, and we fail to see what is unexpected or unpleasant. You and I have marveled at speakers who blithely continue to speak seemingly oblivious to the restless, somnabulant, or hostile responses of their listeners. Such speakers simply illustrate the human tendency to note what we expect and want to note and ignore all else. To combat this tendency we need to remind ourselves that prior analysis is a matter of predicting events before they occur—and predictions are subject to error. Even a weather forecaster watching a massive weather front moving into an area will speak of an "80 percent chance" of nasty weather. Predicting human responses is far less precise; so, we are wise to expect some deviations from expected audience responses.

Process analysis also requires us to shift gears a bit. Up to this point our efforts have been directed toward making our message effective in a particular public communication situation. We examined ourselves, the audience, the context, and the setting as a means of adapting the message. Now, as we begin to watch the speaking encounter unfold, we must prepare ourselves to see as objectively as we can manage, what happens.

Imagine yourself as a very curious, keenly perceptive but uninvolved third party witnessing the encounter. What do you see and hear from such a perspective? One possibility that may not otherwise exist is that you will discover some portion of the audience is not responding to your message at all. An evangelist speaking at a rescue mission and focusing intently on the content and expected outcomes of his message may easily delude himself into thinking that the attention and benign smiles of his auditors are evidence of their agreement with and acceptance of his powerful message. A more objective observer will see the same attention and smiles as predictable responses to a warm room and the promise of a free meal.

To be effective in conducting ongoing analysis of public speaking situations, we must consciously work to defeat our subjectivity, to see what a keen but disinterested observer would see, and, if possible, to alter our presentation to accommodate unforeseen circumstances. Certainly no easy task. You will discover, however, that your conscious efforts to analyze and adjust speaking encounters in this way—even if those efforts are not completely successful—will pay disproportionate dividends.

POSTANALYSIS

I cannot imagine an individual carefully working through the processes of preparing and presenting a speech and then failing to examine the results. Yet failure to analyze speaking encounters after they have concluded is all too common. Indeed, those encounters which achieve some degree of success are less likely to be examined than speaking encounters which fail. We are usually anxious to know why we have failed so that similar, painful experiences can be avoided. But many public speakers are reluctant to scrutinize successful public encounters too closely lest they discover that they were not unalloyed successes or that success was more fortuitous than deserved. Analyzing a presentation following its conclusion can tell us to what extent our purpose for speaking was fulfilled, can reveal strengths and weaknesses in our efforts to analyze and adapt to audiences in particular situations, and can reveal the adequacy of our preparation and practice procedures.

Our first concern, of course, is to learn whether or not we achieved our purpose in speaking. Sometimes this can be quickly ascertained. If my purpose is to persuade people to buy electric zippers, I can determine the success of my persuasive speaking by counting the number of electric zippers purchased. Other purposes require other methods of assessment.

If my purpose in speaking is to provide understanding, I can perhaps question selected members of the audience following the presentation to determine the extent of their understanding. A less direct but equally revealing method of determining the level of an audience's understanding is to invite questions from the audience and then carefully note the kind of questions asked. If the questions refer to matter covered in the presentation, it should be evident that understanding was not achieved. Often the way audience members speak of a topic following a speech reveals their understanding and agreement. Generally, if audience members use words similar to those used by the speaker, if they refer to examples and other supporting materials used by the speaker, and if their subsequent discussions of the topic reflect the organization of ideas used by the speaker, then there is convincing evidence that the speaker achieved understanding and acceptance of his ideas. Therefore, a keen ear is often all a speaker needs to determine whether his purpose has been achieved. Either by direct observation or by careful questioning of others who have access to audience members, experienced speakers will attempt to learn how audience members talk about the speech topic following the presentation.

The methods of determining the results—both immediate and long term—of our public speaking efforts are limited only by time, money, and ingenuity. Most often, if we are really interested in finding out how well we achieved our purpose for speaking, we are likely to find the means to do so.

Postanalysis is also a bit like the stock broker who carefully reviews the stock market at the close of the day to see how accurately predictions were made. Public presentations are constructed and delivered largely on the basis of educated guesses about audiences and situations. Postanalysis can tell us how accurate our guesses were. Did our carefully adapted messages achieve predictable results? If not, why not? What additional data about the audience/situation would have been beneficial? What pieces of information that we did have should we have regarded more importantly than we did? Finally, by reviewing what actually occurred during the encounter, we can make a judgment about how the just-completed encounter will be similar to anticipated encounters. Remember that we once regarded now-familiar speaking situations as strange and perhaps hazardous. Are we likely to be speaking before similar audiences about similar topics under similar circumstances in the future? If so, what we have learned about the audience/situation can assist those later efforts. If not, the specific information we used to adapt to the audience/situation will not be helpful in subsequent efforts. Nevertheless, the procedures we used to gather salient data and incorporate it in preparing and delivering a specifically adapted message will assist subsequent speaking efforts. After all, each speaking opportunity offers unique challenges, despite the similarities they bear to previous speaking encounters.

Postanalysis forces us to review the habits and predilections which direct our efforts to analyze audience/situations and to adapt messages for presentation based on such analysis. While this may sound terribly complex, it need not be. Essentially, you are answering four questions: (1) What did I intend to do? (2) How did I go about preparing to do it? (3) How did it work? (4) What can I learn from this experience that will make the next experience easier and more effective?

SUMMARY

This chapter began simply. I suggested that effective public communication is a matter of accomplishing our purpose by first knowing and then adapting to the particular people and circumstances we are likely to confront. I described three levels of analysis for public speaking: prior, process, and postanalysis. And I argued the value of looking at five interrelated factors that, taken together, make up a speaking situation: speaker, audience, context, setting, and message.

I used the analysis and artful adaptation in *The Music Man* to illustrate several aspects of situational analysis for public speaking and to highlight the interrelationships among these aspects.

I am reminded of a deceptively difficult task I was given some years ago. I was told that I was to provide written instructions to someone trying to get a soft drink out of a vending machine. I was further instructed to assume that that person had never seen or operated a vending machine. What is for most people a simple task became for me complex in the describing. As I described where to put the money, the combination of coins that would and would not work, the mechanism for retrieving change, etc., the simple task took on incredible—and probably unnecessary—complexity. Situational analysis is like that; it is considerably easier to do than it is to describe. A little thought, a little planning, reasonably conscientious effort, a touch of playful creativity, a continuing effort to be objective, and perhaps a little "chutzpah" will go a long way in directing our efforts to analyze and adapt to speaking situations. Harold Hill is a clever character, but he is no genius. He succeeds because he is willing to do what he can to understand and adapt to particular speaking situations. He understands as we must that "knowing the territory" is an essential first step toward success in public encounters.

Notes

1. Willson, M., *The Music Man* (New York: G. P. Putnam's Sons, 1958).

2. Otto, W., and Sagar, A., *Communicating Successfully: How to Give a More Successful Presentation* (Paramus, N.J.: Time-Life Video, 1973).

3. Manchester, W., *Goodbye Darkness: A Memoir of the Pacific War* (Boston: Little, Brown, 1979), 309.

4. Clevenger, T., Jr., *Audience Analysis* (Indianapolis: Bobbs-Merrill, 1966), 13.

5. This is a definition of a reference group suggested in Shibutani, T., "Reference Groups as Perspectives," *American Journal of Sociology*, 60 (May 1955): 562–69.

CHAPTER 4

Making Public Talk: Crafting the Message

Chapter 2 argued that personal, professional, and audience/situation needs, problems, and opportunities bring us to make public discourse. Thus far in this book I have urged you to seek out opportunities for presenting public speeches as often as possible. Students and professional people who have heard me make this spiel tell me that, while they understand what I'm saying and while they agree it is a good idea to seek out speaking opportunities, good speech ideas don't occur to them very often. Further, most of the needs and problems they encounter have been identified and discussed by others; consequently, there seems little more to be said. In short, most of the time they have difficulty finding something worthwhile to say.

THE WELL-INFORMED SPEAKER

Even when they are given a speaking assignment as part of their professional or community responsibilities, they have difficulty thinking of fresh ideas or new approaches to familiar topics. This problem is understandable, widespread, and indicative of major challenges an effective public person must accept. The effective public person must take the trouble to become well-informed on a variety of professional and public matters and must cultivate a genuine curiosity about people, events, and ideas.

Idle Talk

The effective public person understands, for example, the value of idle talk. People talking at bus stops, in supermarket lines, in restaurants, in company cafeterias, at cocktail parties, and at a host of other places say many things about themselves, other people, events, and ideas. Often idle talk is mundane, banal, even boring. But occasionally it yields startling insights, complex analyses, creative thought, and good information. As an aspiring public person, you are likely to find favorite haunts for monitoring idle talk and favorite individuals for sharing idle talk.

I have found, for instance, that janitors are amazingly well-informed about what goes on in the buildings they service. Perhaps they read what they find in wastebaskets and lying about in offices. I'm always impressed at their uncanny ability to predict events before they occur.

The idle talk on radio and television programs may be another source of usable ideas for public speeches. Talk shows, panel discussions, and even popular programming can be productive sources of speech materials.

City garbage collectors often scavenge through the refuse they collect from behind houses and garages, and the result is sometimes considerable extra income from salvaged goods. As effective public persons, we should emulate the spirit of these people: much of what we see and hear is worthless, but if we are willing to look and listen patiently we will be rewarded.

The Printed Word

I would not expect any public speaker to rely exclusively or even substantially upon idle talk; while it may be occasionally helpful, it is not a primary resource for public speakers. The primary resource for generating ideas and fresh insights for public speeches is the printed word. The effective public person must be a voracious reader. I encourage students to engage in two kinds of reading: "Manchurian" reading and "tunnel" reading. Manchurian reading is indiscriminate, wide-ranging, and continuous. The Manchurian reader reads cereal boxes, billboards, match covers, paint cans, bumper stickers, junk mail, trade journals, magazines, newspapers, books, and anything else that is printed and within reach.

You may recall that the film character played by Frank Sinatra in *The Manchurian Candidate* suffered an unusual side effect from the psychological and physical conditioning to which he was subjected as a prisoner of the Chinese during the Korean War. He found himself compelled to read books on all sorts of subjects, subjects he had never suspected would interest him—a truly serious ailment and one which all effective public persons must contract. There is no substitute for reading, and I encourage Manchurian reading, the kind typified by the person who has four books going, subscribes to two daily newspapers, and complains frequently of reading fatigue.

Heavy reading ought to be accompanied by note taking. Good ideas, anecdotes, quotations, and other potential speech material should be noted, cataloged, and filed away for future reference. Often the same piece of material can be used effectively in several different speeches over the years. Comedian Bob Hope understands the value of retaining good material. His home contains a filing system that keeps thousands of jokes from previous performances. Good material is ageless. The introduction of microcomputers offers a modern means of storing and recalling large amounts of material for speeches.

Tunnel reading is focused, intensive reading that occurs after a speaker has chosen a topic for a public presentation. One definition of a good topic for public speaking is that it is something you know well from experience or reading but about which you can discover more. Tunnel reading focuses on the chosen topic or aspects of the audience/situation. For example, a speaker asked to talk to the Bohemian Club about gold prices obviously needs to be well-versed on how gold prices are established and altered by various factors. But the speaker also ought to find

FIGURE 4.1 Building An All-Purpose Speech File

Good material does not readily come to hand at the moment you decide to make a public presentation. You will find it helpful to collect speech ideas, illustrative materials, and exemplary language usage on a continuous basis.

An ordinary file box will do. Keep a stack of appropriate size cards on hand and add continually to your trove of materials. Catalog systems for personal computers may serve the same purpose. Some suggestions you may find helpful are as follows:

1. Make the file uniquely yours. Organize it to suit your needs. You may wish to include: speech ideas that occur to you, examples, anecdotes, illustrations, quotations, striking statistics, and even sample speech outlines.

2. Identify and date all entries so that you can provide complete source information and judge the usefulness of all materials. Speech files, like closets and fishing tackle boxes, require periodic cleaning out.

3. Establish a notation system which will allow you to recall when and for what audience you used the material.

everything possible about the nature, history, purposes, and prevailing values of this extraordinary organization. The combination of monitoring idle talk and Manchurian and tunnel reading will assure public speakers of ample materials for building effective public speeches.

CRAFTING A PUBLIC MESSAGE

You know you have enough materials for a speech when you can't possibly use all the best of it in the time allotted and when you are sure you can answer any question audience members might ask after hearing you speak on the topic. Now you must do what is painful for many people to do: You must reject some material. You will have to resist the tendency to become overly attached to materials you have collected through hard work. Materials must be selected on the basis of three scrupulously applied criteria:

First, you will reject some attractive material for use in the speech because it is not appropriate to the anticipated audience/situation. It may be too complex or too simplistic, too familiar or too novel, too general or too specific. To be effective, speech materials must be carefully adapted to what we know about the audience and the circumstances in which we expect to find them. Perhaps the most common error in this regard is the use of a favorite joke at the beginning of the speech, whether or not it fits the subject matter or the audience/situation. Usually the speaker has used the joke before, discovered people enjoy it, and can't imagine why others wouldn't enjoy hearing it. Audience members may well enjoy the joke but find it difficult to listen to the serious talk that follows immediately. If it doesn't fit the particular audience/situation, it has to go.

Second, if the material does not advance your purpose in speaking it must be rejected. Some information is sure to please or impress some audiences but do nothing to justify its use. I recall an undergraduate class in English literature that was popular on campus. The professor was an accomplished scholar and a marvelous storyteller who loved to tell stories about the years he spent as a combat soldier in Europe during World War II. The class would pay rapt attention while being regaled with stories of heroism, cowardice, tragedy, and triumph—with a humorous anecdote thrown in from time to time for good measure. It was great stuff, but it was not English literature. The effective public speaker must resist the temptation to become caught up in material irrelevant to the decision to speak in the first place.

Finally, even if the material is appropriate to your purpose and meets the requirements of the audience, it must be rejected if it cannot be fitted into the time permitted to you for speaking. Time limits are not safely violated, and the idea that an audience will remain attentive as long as you have something worthwhile to say is a risky half-truth. People will remain interested so long as they think you have something so worth hearing that they can overlook your taking longer than they expected you to take to say it. Some good material will have to be set aside—perhaps to be used to good effect in a question-and-answer session following the speech—simply because you must respect time as a serious audience constraint on your public speaking efforts.

What remains after such often painful winnowing and sifting are the essential remnants from which you will build the talk. Further selection may be necessary as you organize the message, but the essential material is now at hand. As a further check, you may wish to examine the materials you have selected to determine how well they fit your general purpose, the specific purpose, and the residual-message statement you tentatively fashioned earlier. Finally, it may be useful to determine how well this essential remnant meets the adaptive requirements identified by your analysis of the audience/situation. If you are confident that your selection of a topic and materials to support that topic meets the tests suggested to this point, you are ready to begin organizing the message.

Organizing the Talk

One of the most severe criticisms that can be made of a professional person is that he is disorganized. Often such a criticism refers as much to habits of mind as well as habits of work. Organization is essential to effective work of all kinds, and it is critical to effective public speaking.

You and I organize first because we want to clarify and control our own thought processes. Until we see how ideas fit together, how one idea reinforces or expands a previous idea, and how ideas march to a conclusion, we do not know our subject as well as we can. We have also had the experience of discovering something interesting and important in the process of organizing our thoughts; a relationship we had not suspected may be made obvious to us, or an alternate view of a concept may be suggested when the concept is framed among other ideas and concepts. Organizing is something we do for ourselves, and it is essential for that reason. We must also organize because listeners demand it.

In public communication encounters, listeners will usually struggle to overcome inherent obstacles. First, they cannot control the pace at which information is presented to them. A conversational rate is about 160 to 180 words per minute. If something is missed or misunderstood, it is unlikely that it will be clarified. Like Chaplinesque characters, the audience can only watch and listen with growing concern as ideas and information continue to flow past them like cakes on an assembly line. Second, audience members must do a kind of mental juggling act in order to see relationships among ideas. If the first idea presented is related to the third idea presented, that relationship will be apparent to listeners only if they recall Idea 1 as they hear Idea 3. And audiences are often asked to absorb a number of apparently disparate ideas until a conclusion is presented at the end of the presentation. Finally, audience members do not know as they begin to listen to a public speech which ideas are important and which are less important. They must depend upon the speaker to provide the means for distinguishing major thoughts from minor ones. Audiences demand help from the speaker; they demand that the speaker organize what is presented to them. Two distinguished speech communication scholars have summarized these demands as follows:

> Audiences insist that they be helped to understand what a speaker says. Their insistence is partial expression of their natural wish to see the interrelationships among ideas; to see which ideas are primary and which are subsidiary; to detect the rationale behind the overall pattern of a speech. When you depart from an order of thought anticipated by your listeners, or from an apparently logical order of thoughts, you had better explain why; otherwise your hearer will find the flow of thought chaotic. He may suspect you of deliberately trying to mislead.[1]

Public communicators organize to assist themselves to know their material and to present it more effectively. In Chapter 5 we will examine the importance of having a well-organized presentation to assist our efforts in practicing and actually presenting the speech.

The relationship between effective public communication and good organization is like the relationship between an impressive and functional building and the blueprints that guided its construction. Without the blueprints, the building could not have been constructed, but those who admire and use the building need not see the blueprints of even one structural detail. Organization must be sufficiently evident to meet listeners' needs and demands, but not so evident that it detracts from the primary reason for the encounter.

We have all heard speakers present talks with oppressively obvious organization. Each major point is identified by number, and all subpoints are previewed after each major point: "Now, in support of Point 3, let me offer two observations." Worse, each relationship is referred to by the numbers: "As you can see, Point 5 illustrates again the argument for lower interest rates suggested in Points 1 and 3." Such speeches are typically met with pained expressions and clenched teeth. Good speech organization, like small children at a formal dinner, should be seen but not heard.

The selection of an organizational format is guided by the subject matter, the audience/situation, and the purpose in speaking. These considerations, taken together, should lead to the selection of an appropriate and effective organizational plan.

The subject matter of public speeches often dictates the organizational pattern to be used. A talk about water resources in America will lend itself to spatial organization, and a talk on the impact of interest rates upon unemployment will require some kind of cause-effect structure.

Your own research of a subject will frequently reveal how a speech on that subject should be organized. How do informed sources approach and explicate the subject? Will some particular organizational pattern allow you to provide a complete treatment of the subject matter? These criteria may force you to rethink favored or habitual patterns of organizing speeches and may challenge you to find an appropriate organizational pattern for a subject that is unfamiliar, difficult, or badly organized by those who have discussed it previously.

Your purpose in speaking should also guide your selection of an organizational format. If, for example, you wish to illustrate the capriciousness and unnecessary costs of urban zoning regulations, you need not develop a tight legal brief that proves with mathematical precision a causal relationship between poorly conceived zoning regulations and unnecessary costs to businesses and residences. Your purpose is well served if you offer enough examples to convince reasonable people that you are correct in your observations and conclusions. And of course you have to work with the organizational format you choose. If the format you choose is overly complex or bizarre, you are apt to have as much difficulty managing it as your audience will have following it. Ask yourself what you are trying to achieve through interaction with the anticipated audience, and select an organizational format that allows you to do it.

Audience/situation considerations should be allowed to influence the selection of an organizational format. Audiences often develop particular expectations about how particular subjects will be treated. Stockholders attending an annual meeting may expect to hear about dividend income and changes in net worth before learning about new product development and new additions to upper management. Those expectations must be met, or the speaker risks confusing or angering the audience.

Some situations clearly invite particular organizational formats. Dedications and other ceremonial events typically invite the speaker to convey a sense of historical perspective by dealing with events chronologically. The annual State of the Union message by the president of the United States virtually demands that the president follow an organizational pattern that moves from a discussion of accomplishment to the identification of problems and proposals for their remedy.

No organizational pattern is appropriate to all speech topics, all speaker purposes, and all audience/situations. Effective public communication is a continuous exercise in adaptation, of tailoring the message to fit particular requirements. The number of organizational formats available to us is more than sufficient to allow us to choose one that meets all of the criteria discussed here.

Beyond that, you will find it useful from time to time to combine two or more standard organizational patterns or try a variation of a familiar pattern. I find it refreshing to hear a speaker use a chronological format that begins *in medias res.* An open, inventive mind and a determination to make the organizational format work can make the speaking encounter effective and satisfying. To assist your selection, I offer the following short list of common organizational formats, with occasional suggestions about how they may be combined or varied to meet the demands imposed by particular subjects and particular audience/situations.

The *topical* pattern is perhaps the most frequently used and frequently abused organizational format. The topical pattern is an arbitrary selection of elements pertaining to a particular subject. If the subject is the internal-combustion engine, I might talk about the fuel pump, the carburetor, the cam shaft, and the exhaust system. I might just as easily talk about the pistons, the differential gear, the lubrication system, and the ignition system. There is no necessary order among the various elements. While the topical pattern does not lend itself to speeches which purport to offer careful and systematic analysis of a subject, it is widely adaptable to most subject areas.

The trouble is that the topical system is often perceived as a license to ignore audience and other demands. While it offers the speaker wide choice, the topical pattern must be structured to meet the psychological demands of particular audiences as well as the speaker's objectives. Audiences demand that speakers provide a sense of progression as well as topical variety; they must sense that the talk is getting somewhere and is providing reasonably comprehensive treatment of the subject matter. The topical pattern, then, is not entirely an arbitrary selection of elements pertaining to a subject. Rather, it is an organizational pattern which invites selection of those elements of a subject most likely to satisfy the speaker's objectives and the demands of the audience/situation.

Americans are creatures of time. We measure the quality, efficiency, and meaning of our lives in minutes, hours, weeks, and years. We are addicted to wristwatches and clocks; they tell us not only where we are but who we are. Organizing speeches by reference to *time* is, for us, as natural as sleep. Recounting the precise sequence of events can reveal insights, clarify understandings, and point to inescapable conclusions. How many detective yarns have you read which revolve around a careful reconstruction of the accounts by several suspects of how they used their time during a particular period? Processes are often best discussed by describing what happens from first to last. ("To recall Segment 12 without erasing the entire entry, you must first enter the unit code, followed by the 3-digit segment code and then the PARSIM retrieval notation.")

Since past events illuminate the present and assist prediction of the future, a time pattern often begins with the related events most removed in time and moves to the present before projecting into the future. While this is familiar, it is not always necessary. Audiences yearn for variety, especially the kind of variation that titillates without confusing or offending. I recently worked with an executive who was to make a difficult presentation to a regional meeting of company salespersons. A major administrative restructuring had just been completed; a marginally profitable subsidiary had been sold; and rumors of serious financial difficulties were plentiful, although the company was in solid condition.

To simply deny the rumors was unsatisfactory, since such an approach would likely lend some credence to them. Rather, the executive began by offering his listeners a series of predictions about the immediate future of the company, framing his predictions in the form of confident wagers on specific aspects of production and earnings. From these bets, he moved to an explanation of what the company had done to make such predictions possible. Finally, he briefly reviewed current, critical events which demonstrated the wisdom of the company's past actions and suggested that his earlier predictions were more conservative than risky. His success was evident in the relieved smiles that began to appear and the jubilant response that erupted as he concluded. Organizing messages on the basis of time is a familiar and potentially effective technique, especially if you are willing to be a bit creative in how you invite your listeners to view past, present, and future.

Some subjects are best organized using a *spatial* pattern that suggests both the relationships among various parts and the configuration of the whole as it exists in space. Bone structure may be better understood if we note that the head bone is connected to the neck bone, the neck bone to the shoulder bone, etc. Most of us learned geography by finding our home town and home state on a map or globe and then working our way from there to the far reaches of the planet. Spatial arrangement works because it proceeds in understandable directions, allowing listeners to know at any given moment where they have been, where they are, and where they are headed. We move from east to west, from top to bottom, and from inside to outside. Movement can be made in any direction so long as a unifying configuration or idea guides that movement and allows you to accomplish your purpose by projecting an appropriate figure-ground relationship at each point.

Occasionally, you may delay revealing the total picture to build tension and interest as you proceed, but this must be done with the realization that audience members vary in their abilities to tolerate tension. I may describe an automobile beginning at the hood ornament and moving to the trailer hitch without mentioning that I am describing a Rolls Royce, but my listeners are likely to get a better picture and be better satisfied if I do mention early that it is a Rolls Royce.

Because public speakers often confront audiences to resolve problems, the *problem-solution* format is popular and broadly appropriate. In its simplest form, the speaker presents a problem to the audience and offers a solution which is both practical and desirable. If there is reason to believe that the audience is unfamiliar with the problem, unconvinced of its importance, or hostile to the suggestion that a problem truly exists, the speaker should devote most of the available time to clarifying the problem or establishing its credibility and urgency. If, on the other hand, the audience is familiar with the problem and is convinced of its urgency, time will be better spent identifying and arguing the merits of the solution.

Some years ago, a colleague and friend who taught in the school of agriculture at a midwestern university became involved in efforts to control Johnson grass. Farm groups to which he spoke were well aware of the danger this tough weed posed to food crops. He needed only to mention the problem and outline a comprehensive program for eradication involving cooperative efforts between farmers and the staff of the agriculture school, with funding from public and private sources. To ensure support for the necessary funding legislation, he spoke to a number of citizen groups. For them, he spoke at length about the problem posed by Johnson grass and how it affected the prices each member of the audience had to pay for food; only briefly did he outline the solution. He then concluded by asking for their support. Like other organizational formats, the problem-solution pattern is best employed with careful attention to prevailing audience/situation requirements.

Assume that an audience is well informed on an issue or problem but is having difficulty deciding what direction to take or which solution is apt to be most practical and desirable. This audience/situation is best served by a *forced-choice* organizational pattern. Here, the speaker carefully enumerates the criteria which should guide the selection of a solution. This is followed by a review of the most frequently offered solutions using the just-cited criteria. Solutions are eliminated systematically as they are shown to violate one or more of the criteria. Finally, a solution is offered which meets all of the criteria.

Four distinct hazards attend the use of the forced-choice format. First, the listeners must agree with you about the nature, relevance, and urgency of the issue or problem being discussed. Second, they must accept the criteria for a solution that you offer; the listeners must feel that your criteria are comprehensive and fair. Third, audience members must agree that you have identified the most representative solutions proffered by serious people. To ignore a solution that the audience knows about and considers reasonable if not perfect is to risk failure of the entire effort. Finally, listeners must agree that you have applied the criteria evenly and objectively in eliminating all solutions but one.

Matters of public policy are particularly amenable to the forced-choice organizational pattern. Milwaukee has recently confronted the problem of renovating its metropolitan sewage treatment system. Various options, each with impressive price tags, have been offered by citizen groups, environmental groups, professional engineers, and a consulting firm. The forced-choice format has been repeatedly applied in public presentations and hearings to determine what methods of construction and financing are most practical and desirable. Unfortunately, no solution has been chosen, because competing spokespersons have largely failed to recognize and respond to the first hazard cited above; the citizens of the Milwaukee area have not been convinced that a problem requiring immediate attention and the expenditure of hundreds of millions of dollars exists. The forced-choice format is appropriate in many situations in which choices must be made among potential solutions, but its success depends upon the skill with which it is applied and the extent to which listener-generated hazards can be avoided.

The *cause-effect* pattern also points to a particular solution or conclusion, but it does so by suggesting a cause-effect relationship that must inform any solution or conclusion. Typically, the pattern begins with an enumeration of effects that are alleged to be evident and in some way harmful. This is followed by the citation of causes which have produced the effects and, if altered, will result in the elimination of the undesirable effects. Clearly, the second step is critical here. There must be convincing evidence that a clear relationship exists between cause and effect, that the alleged cause is sufficient to produce the effect, and that no other causes are responsible for the effect.

In the 1980 presidential campaign, Ronald Reagan pointed to government spending for social programs and regulation as the cause for mounting federal deficits and double-digit inflation. If social programs were restricted to the truly needy and if regulatory activity was restrained, he argued, federal deficits would be eliminated within four years, inflation would be controlled, federal taxes could be cut, and economic prosperity would result. Political presentations often follow a cause-effect format, and incumbents are generally held to be responsible for any problems which exist at election time. If the speaker can be sufficiently persuasive in convincing an audience that particular causes produce particular effects, then the cause-effect format will prove effective. This pattern has the additional advantage of being comparatively easy for the speaker to manage and easy for the listeners to follow, since it typically includes only three sharply demarcated steps.

The *Monroe Motivated Sequence*[2] is a psychologically based, highly adaptable organizational format developed by Professor Alan H. Monroe of Purdue University. Dr. Monroe attempted to determine the audience needs which would have to be successively satisfied if public discourse were to succeed. Further, he sought to produce a format which could be easily adapted to particular situational factors as they were revealed through audience/situation analysis. The result was the Motivated Sequence, which includes five steps: First, attention must be present or it must be gained by the speaker; second, unless the audience is already aware of the nature and urgency of a problem or need for change, the speaker must establish such a need or problem; third, the speaker must offer a course of action which satisfies the need or remedies the problem;

fourth, listeners must be led to visualize what good will result if the recommended course of action is adopted or what harm will result if the course of action is rejected; finally, the speaker will appeal directly for specific action.

The value of the motivated sequence as an organizational scheme lies in its adaptability. Monroe did not intend for it to be used in a rigid or simplistic way; rather, it was designed to anticipate audience/situation demands and respond to them. Each step reminds us of what must be present in the audience/situation or must be supplied by the speaker. For example, it is hardly necessary to argue that public speaking will not succeed if the speaker does not gain and retain the attention of the audience. It is obvious, however, that some subjects and occasions virtually guarantee attention. A quarterback facing a fourth down and goal with two seconds left in a game his team is losing by four points hardly needs to begin his address in the huddle by saying, "Let me have your attention." Often what needs to be present *is* present and need not occupy the time and talk of the speaker. But unless the speaker has good reasons to believe that the audience/situation supplies what is needed, he must discover the means to provide it.

All steps in the motivated sequence can be abbreviated, expanded, or eliminated as necessary. Consider, for example, a company president who addresses his employees following a public announcement that the company has been acquired by a conglomerate with headquarters in another city. Attention by his listeners can be safely assumed, and the discussion of the need or problem can be abbreviated. If the employees are reasonably familiar with the terms of the merger, the satisfaction step can be similarly short. The bulk of the president's time can be devoted to discussing the implications of the merger, pointing out the ways in which employees will be affected and perhaps asking for particular behavior from his listeners, even if it is only to continue to work as if nothing had happened. Because the Monroe Motivated Sequence is based upon the psychological requirements of audiences, and because it is adaptable to any situational requirement, it can be an organizational format of first or last resort.

Selecting an appropriate organizational format is a matter of choosing from among a large number of available schemes. The seven formats discussed here are only the most common organizational patterns used for public speaking. Others, like the ascending-descending pattern, the reflective sequence, and the refutational pattern could be used, and many familiar patterns can be creatively altered to suit particular requirements. Two or more organizational patterns may be combined, especially for longer messages that present special problems and opportunities. You are only as limited as your imagination and daring in selecting an organizational pattern that suits your purpose, your subject matter, and the particular audience/situation requirements that you confront. The best test of an organizational pattern is that it allows you to do in any given audience/situation what you wish to do.

Introductions and Conclusions

Now that you know what you want to talk about in public and why and to whom and under what circumstances you will do it, and now that you have decided how you will organize what you have to say, you can consider how to introduce and conclude the speech. There is not much point in planning an introduction and a conclusion until you know what is to be introduced and concluded. Introductions and conclusions are no less important for being considered late in the process of message preparation. Many an outstanding speech has failed because audience interest and the speaker's credibility were destroyed by a bungled introduction, and otherwise worthy efforts have achieved‧ only middling success because of a botched conclusion.

Generally the introduction and the conclusion together should not exceed 25 percent of the total speaking time. The bulk of the time must be reserved for the body of the speech; nevertheless, a number of important tasks must be accomplished in both the introduction and the conclusion. Four tasks, for instance, must be completed in the introduction. The speaker must (1) gain favorable and sustainable attention, (2) establish personal credibility with the listeners, (3) provide sufficient background information and organizational cues to assist listeners in their efforts to understand the message, and (4) acknowledge and adapt as necessary to the occasion. Let us examine each of these tasks in turn.

As we noted earlier in discussing the Monroe Motivated Sequence, the speaker's purpose cannot be accomplished without the attention of the audience. But mere attention is not enough. Attention can be gained in a variety of ways, some decidedly inappropriate. A student in my public speaking class some years ago began a speech by removing his pants. Despite the fact that his speech concerned water skiing techniques, his opening stunt so shocked and distracted his audience that he accomplished very little. Many years ago, a masterful scholar of public communication, James A. Winans,[3] spoke of gaining "fair" attention, the kind of attention that is stimulating without being shocking, inviting without being flashy. Such attention is more likely to sustain throughout the entire presentation.

A number of empirical studies of speech communication[4] have demonstrated that audiences make critical judgments about the expertise, honesty, and personal commitment of the speaker within the first few moments of the presentation. Unless they regard the speaker as credible before the presentation, members of the audience will look and listen for something which will help them decide whether or not to accept the speaker and what the speaker has to say. If you have any reason to doubt that your listeners will regard you as sufficiently credible to speak effectively on your topic, you must attempt to establish your credibility as part of the introduction. This may be accomplished in a variety of ways. If you have appropriate credentials and relevant experiences that are unknown to your listeners, you may briefly review those credentials and experiences. If you can do it without becoming tedious, you may review your preparation, pointing out the sources of your information and the research you have conducted. Beyond such direct efforts, you should not overlook the credibility that is often gained by simply appearing and sounding confident. In the following chapter we will take a close look at speech delivery. Suffice it to note at this point that direct eye contact, good vocal qualities, and effective body control are nowhere more important than at the beginning of the presentation.

A good introduction attracts the listeners to the topic and encourages them to listen further. A first question that listeners have that must be answered promptly at the risk of failure of the encounter is "What has all of this got to do with me?" Another way to frame the question, which indicates the risks that the speaker runs early in the presentation, is "Why should these listeners want to stay in their seats for the next few seconds?" You must provide information that satisfies such concerns. To do so, you may reveal the reasons that brought you to regard the topic as important and urgent enough to speak publicly. If the matter is unfamiliar to your listeners, you may review background information and relevant history, define key terms, and relate examples which illustrate the relevance of the topic to your listeners. ("You may never have heard of Johnson grass; and, if you have, you may not have considered it worth your attention. But I intend to prove to you that you can't afford to ignore the problem of Johnson grass. It threatens the food you eat.")

Unfamiliar material is often difficult for listeners to process. Consequently, they require more than the usual speech structuring. Previewing the organization of the speech will often remedy difficulties and prevent the listeners from becoming confused at the outset. Or you may find it useful to assure the listeners that while the subject may be initially confusing, clarification will follow quickly if they will bear with you. Obviously, you should not place unwarranted demands upon the patience or intellectual capacities of your listeners. Your task is to entice them to remain attentive and want to hear more.

Finally, a good introduction will acknowledge and adapt as necessary. You may sometime find yourself speaking publicly on an occasion made meaningful by extraneous circumstances. If you are speaking on Labor Day or during National Pickle Week, you may be expected to acknowledge the importance of the occasion and demonstrate how your talk is influenced by and reflects the moment.

An introduction can be as brief as a few words or as long as several minutes. You will confront a number of potential obstacles at the outset of any speech. You dare not assume attention and interest from your listeners. They may not be prepared or favorably disposed to hear what you have to say; on the other hand, an audience may be highly motivated by circumstances, previous experiences, or personal predilections to hear all of what you say. Consider the following example. The movie *Patton* opened with a stunning speech by General Patton, played by George C. Scott. An audience of uniformed soldiers stood in neat rows facing a high stage with nothing on it. At the rear of the stage an enormous American flag overwhelmed the scene. The general appeared on stage wearing a uniform replete with decorations and accented by highly polished boots, two pearl-handled pistols, and a helmet with a mirrorlike gleam. In two words he accomplished all that he needed to accomplish in introducing his talk. He said, "Be seated."

The function of the conclusion is to provide a satisfactory end to the speaking encounter. Your listeners want to know, usually somewhat in advance, that the speech is drawing to a close in a satisfactory manner. This can be accomplished in a variety of ways. The most common conclusion is succinct summary of the major ideas presented in the speech. The summary can be made more effective if it is augmented by the residual message; listeners have an opportunity to see how the main points of the speech support and illustrate the most critical idea in the speech.

The conclusion may also provide the most appropriate opportunity to call for action by the listeners. This is the time to be specific about what behavior is desired of the listeners. If you have been speaking on behalf of the United Fund drive, the conclusion is the time to ask your listeners to fill out and return pledge cards. One of the most common errors made by public speakers who speak to achieve specific action from their listeners is the tendency to be vague and hesitant in asking for specific action and commitment. Sales managers understand the problem all too well. Sales trainees who are bright, knowledgeable, and otherwise capable often seem unable to close a sales presentation by asking for a decision to purchase. Skilled presentations fail unnecessarily because the salesman is unwilling to ask for the specific decision the entire speech is intended to elicit.

Other means of concluding the presentation include references to the purposes, the examples, and the statements identified in the introduction. Listeners are thus provided with a sense of cohesion and completeness which may be difficult to achieve otherwise. ("I said at the outset that I would show you the most common but least-noticed form of child neglect. There can be no doubt that inattention to the nutritional needs of small children is a dangerous form of child neglect which is easily ignored—even encouraged.")

Introductions and conclusions do not typically occupy much of our time in public speaking, but effectiveness in public speaking often depends upon how well these critical parts of the speech are managed.

The listeners, the subject matter, or the speaking context may simplify or complicate what must be done in beginning or ending the speech. You can be sure, however, that your efforts to discover what the speaking situation requires you to do in introducing and concluding the speech and your efforts to meet those requirements intelligently and imaginatively will pay handsome dividends.

Fleshing Out the Message

It is essential that the speech be carefully structured, but that alone is hardly sufficient. Each major idea, each argument, each conclusion in the speech structure must be amplified and supported. The quality of the supporting materials will determine whether or not listeners will be interested, will understand, will agree, or will wish to act upon what you say. Supporting materials develop the message; they give the message interest, liveliness, relevance, credibility, clarity, and persuasive impact. There are many kinds of supporting materials from which to choose in achieving your purpose, and your success in building and presenting an attractive and effective message will depend upon your willingness to ferret out and use only the best, the most suitable, and the most compelling. From the winnowing and sifting process described earlier in this chapter, you must select a plentiful and varied supply of supporting materials that are appropriate to your purpose, the subject matter, the particular audience, the anticipated circumstances. Then the best of these will be used to develop and support the speech.

A review of the most commonly used forms of support, together with an explanation of how they can be used most effectively, may assist your efforts to build more attractive and effective messages. Two major criteria, however, should guide your selection and use of supporting materials: the materials should be well adapted to your purpose and the audience/situation, and the materials should be as varied as you can manage.

Audiences rarely tolerate a high level of abstraction for very long; listeners will demand that you be specific. For this reason examples, illustrations, and anecdotes are effective forms of support. An example is a specific instance which shows in detail the character or nature of something else. Courage, for example, is difficult to explain, but I can help an audience understand it if I point to the example of a fourteen-year-old boy in Indiana who crawled under an overturned and burning truck to pull his unconscious older brother to safety. The example is brief but concrete.

Illustrations and anecdotes, on the other hand, are elaborated examples told in narrative and especially concrete form. As far as possible they include names, dates, places, and other detail. People enjoy a good story, especially if they can see themselves—their experiences, values, and emotions—in the story. The well-chosen illustration or anecdote, perhaps more than any other kind of supporting material, adds interest, vividness, and persuasive impact to the public speech.

Note the detail, the spine-tingling tension, and the compelling human emotion in this illustration of human courage told by Elmer Bendiner. Bendiner was a navigator in an American B-17 bomber during the early days of World War II. A particular menace were 20-mm shells fired by German fighters. These shells were designed to pierce the fuel tanks of the bombers and then explode, turning the fortress into a mass of flames. In a raid on Kassel, Germany, in July 1943, Bendiner was on board the *Tondelayo*, which was piloted by a man named Bohn. The aircraft was savagely attacked by German fighters over the target, lost two waist gunners, and was hit by what appeared to the crew to be 20-mm shells. The plane did not explode, and the crew managed to return to England and land safely.

Upon inspection, the fuel tanks were found to contain eleven unexploded 20-mm shells. Later, a captain of intelligence swore the pilot to secrecy and told him what had been discovered when armorers opened each of the shells taken from the fuel tank. Bendiner writes:

> They were as clean as whistles and as harmless. Empty? Not quite, said the captain, tantalizing Bohn as Bohn tantalized me. One was not empty. It contained a carefully rolled piece of paper. On it was a scrawl in Czech. The intelligence captain had scoured Kimbolton for a man who could read Czech. . . . Translated the note read: "This is all we can do for you now."[5]

A good illustration is often worth volumes of definitions and explanations.

The illustration above is a true story; notice how the names, dates, places, and other concrete detail make it interesting and believable. But illustrations and anecdotes can be factual or hypothetical. To be effective you must choose illustrations and anecdotes relevant to the points you are attempting to clarify and support, and your listeners must see each illustration and anecdote as a credible representation of reality. Your listeners will be quick to notice if you are stretching a point or being farfetched, and they will tolerate such talk only if they feel you are attempting to be humorous or clearly wish not to be taken seriously.

Finding good, vivid, detailed, and directly relevant illustrations and anecdotes is one of the most difficult challenges you confront in your efforts to become an effective public communicator. The value of Manchurian reading may be more evident to you now, because such reading is most often the source of usable illustrations and anecdotes. And you will find that collecting them continuously is wise; they seem particularly difficult to find on short notice.

Personal experiences, particularly if they are somewhat unusual and relevant, can add liveliness and credibility to your public messages. The primary value of personal experience is that it demonstrates your personal involvement and investment with the subject matter. As indicated earlier, listeners want to know how you are personally involved with and committed to your subject. After all, if you are not involved or committed, why should they accept your invitation to become involved or committed? Personal experiences, used credibly and judiciously, positively answer this question for listeners and give your speech special impact.

Most of you would be as interested as I was some time ago in listening to a young man present a speech urging the audience to take free classes in cardiopulmonary resuscitation. He began by noting that we had probably heard pitches for CPR training before and agreed it would be nice to take such classes someday. "Don't wait for someday," he urged, "You may need CPR sooner than you think. I'm lucky. I took CPR training in September of last year, and completed the training in early October. Five days later, I used my CPR training to revive my father when he collapsed in the parking lot of County Stadium following a football game. Don't wait to learn how you can save the life of someone close to you. Take CPR training now!"

Quotations are an effective method of borrowing credibility for public speeches. Most audiences do not expect you to know all there is to know about a subject, and there are few situations in which you can expect to influence audience attitudes and beliefs on the strength of your personal credibility. Quotations are useful in filling the gaps in your credibility with a particular audience. This is done by using quotations to demonstrate the extensiveness and quality of your research and the extent to which other individuals, regarded as credible by your listeners, agree with what you say. It might appear, for example, quite modern to argue the strength of the "democratic" family as opposed to the traditional, autocratic family model with the father as the autocrat and the line of authority moving down to the mother and then to older children, with the youngest child having the least authority. The argument takes on a different perspective, however, if the following, written before the turn of the century, is used. Theodore Roosevelt wrote:

> To all who have known really happy family lives; that is to all who have known or who have witnessed the greatest happiness which there can be on this earth, it is hardly necessary to say that the highest idea of the family is attainable only where the father and mother stand to each other as lovers and friends. In these homes, the children are bound to father and mother by ties of love, respect, and obedience, which are simply strengthened by the fact that they are treated as reasonable beings with rights of their own, and that the rule of the household is changed to suit the changing years, as childhood passes into manhood and womanhood.[6]

The speaker who used this quotation profited not only from the endorsement of a respected historical figure but from the fact that the quotation adds the weight of historical perspective to the present argument. Listeners are more apt to accept ideas which have been advanced by authoritative individuals over some period of time. In addition, this quotation adds particular definition to what is meant by a democratic family.

Definitions are used to clarify unfamiliar terms and concepts; they are based upon authority, behavior, operation, and, of course, etymology and common usage. Take the word "exigency," for instance. A dictionary definition reads "urgent need; emergency." This is based upon the Latin word *exigentia*, meaning "need."

As an example of the use of authority in definitions, especially useful when referring to specialized definitions of familiar words or concepts, we can cite the published work of Professor Lloyd Bitzer of the University of Wisconsin, Madison, who defines a rhetorical or communicative exigency as "a need, problem, deficiency, or opportunity marked by a sense of urgency which can be resolved in whole or in part by communication."[7]

Defining words and concepts in terms of observable behavior is particularly effective, since it invites listeners to associate new words and concepts with observable or familiar behavior. An old Army maxim is, "If it doesn't have stripes and moves, salute it; it's an officer."

To define terms or concepts operationally is to describe a specific, characteristic process. The American vice-president has been defined as a person who receives notable support for high office, assists the election of the president, is assigned a number of seemingly important tasks, and then disappears into political limbo. Operational definitions, like behavioral definitions, have the advantage of pointing to something directly observable or testable. Some technical terms are best defined operationally. Dieseling, for instance, is defined as the continuation of combustion in gasoline engines after the ignition has been turned off.

Statistics summarize large amounts of data in numerical form. Statistics can indicate comparisons, relationships, and central tendencies. Economic prosperity, for example, is measured by increases and decreases in the gross national product (GNP) compared to previous years. Percentage figures are comparisons relating to some base that is presumably known to listeners. If the price of a home computer is described as 20 percent less than the usual price, the presumption is that the usual price is familiar; a percentage increase is meaningful only if the base is known. A department chairman, for example, announced at a meeting with the dean that his department had experienced a 100 percent increase in the number of majors in the department. As other chairpersons nodded appreciatively, the dean quietly asked how many new majors that represented. The chairman smiled and replied, "Two!"

Ratios and correlations are among statistics which indicate the relationship of one thing to another. Often these statistics are used as measures of efficiency, productivity, or effectiveness. If the ratio of profit to waste is 5 to 1, efficiency is indicated. A major-league baseball pitcher is considered effective if he strikes out three batters for every one he walks.

Correlations suggest the closeness of two independent factors. A correlation may be a convincing statistic when it is not possible to show a direct causal relationship. For example, if I can show a high correlation between motorcycle driving and serious injury, I may convince you to avoid buying or riding on a motorcycle even though a direct causal relationship between motorcycle use and injuries may be impossible to draw. After all, not everyone who owns and drives a motorcycle suffers an injury.

Other statistics show central tendencies. The average usually refers to the arithmetic mean, or the number that results when the total of all figures is divided by the number of figures. If 8,000 employees collectively contribute enough money to buy an airplane which costs $4.2 million dollars, the average contribution would be $525.00 The average figure here may not coincide with the contribution of any actual employee (some will have given more and some less), but it may be a good indication of the approximate contribution of each employee. If we want more precise information about the range of individual contributions, we might select the median, that figure which is at the midpoint of the range. For example, if 4,000 people gave less than $495 and 4,000 people gave more than $495, the median figure would be $495. Finally, if we were interested in the amount contributed by the largest number of people, we would look for the mode. If 26 people each gave $621, and if that is the largest number of people contributing the same amount, then $621 would be the mode.

This exercise illustrates how statistics can be used to show different things. If you wish to establish and sustain your credibility as a public speaker, you must learn to select the statistic which is the most representative statistic available. Further, you must remember that statistics are intended to allow you to summarize data, but in doing so you may lose the flavor and the human interest found in the data. I may speak of a 17-percent increase in the survival rate from leukemia, but that cold figure cannot reflect the ectasy and relief of a family that learns their eight-year-old has been successfully treated for leukemia.

Numbers tend to be pretty boring and a bit scary for most people. If you insist on reciting one statistic after another you risk losing the interest and support of your listeners. Statistics are best used like tabasco sauce in a good stew; a dash will do. It is the variety of ingredients and the way they are blended that makes the flavor.

Factual information fills our public messages, but few people appear to know how to distinguish among facts, inferences, or value statements. If I say that the Penn State football team is the most consistently outstanding major college team in the nation, that is a statement that represents my opinion. If, however, I say that the Penn State football team has been ranked among the top ten teams in the nation more often than any other team over the last fifteen years, that is a fact. The difference, of course, is that the latter statement can be verified, while the first statement is unverifiable.

Statements that cannot be verified often function like facts in public discourse. If listeners believe what you say is factual—even if it cannot be verified—it functions as a fact. The reverse, unfortunately, is also true. If listeners choose not to believe that what you have presented is factual, then what you say cannot function as a fact; it will not explain, illustrate, or prove the points you wish to make.

Sometimes direct verification of factual information is not possible. Historical facts, for example, cannot be directly verified because we cannot replay past events; even those videotaped replays can capture only part of athletic events. If I state that during the second Lincoln-Douglas debate Abraham Lincoln wore a stovepipe hat seven inches high, I cannot directly verify that fact. Lincoln may have had such a hat, but he also may have worn one of his other stovepipe hats on the occasion of the second debate with Senator Douglas. A photograph showing Lincoln and Douglas on a debate platform with Lincoln wearing a stovepipe may be questioned: "Is that a picture of the second or the fourth debate?" Even if a historian produced a document signed by Lincoln indicating he had worn a seven-inch stovepipe, its authenticity may be questioned; and, of course, Lincoln may have been mistaken. Where facts cannot be directly verified, we rely heavily upon authoritative sources—sources we regard as credible and likely to be viewed as credible by the listeners.

If you rely upon sources to support the factual information you present, you must cite the sources. If I state that home mortgage foreclosures increased 40 percent during 1981, I would be wise to cite the Federal Deposit Insurance Corporation as the source of the information unless the listeners regard the information as obvious or trust me as a reliable source or have some other reason to believe the statement is correct. We ought to review the factual information we use in public discourse carefully to determine how and how well it will meet the tests that listeners impose upon the facts they hear. As a rule of thumb, you are better advised to err in the direction of qualifying the factual information you present rather than counting on your listeners to accept passively what you offer.

Audiovisual Aids

Audiovisual aids often are parts of professional presentations. I do not wish to suggest that audiovisual aids are not forms of support for the message you present, but I do believe they are overused in public presentations and are often badly used even when they are appropriately a part of the message. I want to sound a cautionary note against the widespread and indiscriminate use of audiovisual aids. My argument, based upon experiences with professional people, is that audiovisual aids are especially seductive. More than any form of support, they are likely to be selected for use for the wrong reasons and used badly during the presentation.

Audiovisual aids, like other forms of support, must be selected to fit the unique requirements of each speaking situation. If the audiovisual aid does not illustrate, clarify, amplify, or otherwise complement the message, it should not be used. Further, because audiovisual aids must be managed by the speaker and because they are things that share the platform with the speaker, they compete with the speaker for the attention of the listeners. When they are used, audiovisual aids temporarily divert attention to some degree from the speaker. The speaker must recapture the complete attention of the audience after audiovisual aids have been used. For these reasons, audiovisual aids must be used judiciously. Indeed, in view of the frequent abuse of audiovisual aids, I urge that they not be used unless they are essential to the success of the public encounter.

When you must use audiovisual aids, ask yourself these questions to insure that you use them properly: First, is the audiovisual aid appropriate to the audience/situation? Does it illustrate or reinforce some specific aspect of the message? Since it complements the message, the audiovisual aid must be well adapted to your purpose and to the special requirements of the speaking situation.

Second, is the audiovisual aid clear? If the aid is visual, it should be large enough to be seen by all members of the audience. It should be uncluttered and attractive. If complex material must be shown, it is better to use several visuals rather than confuse the audience with a visual bristling with information. If an audio aid is used by itself or in conjunction with a visual aid, it should be loud enough for all audience members to hear and of sufficient quality to allow all necessary sound distinctions to be made.

Third, is the audiovisual aid well prepared? Public speakers are routinely urged to avoid hastily prepared, sloppy, or worn audiovisual aids. You should use only clean, colorful, and impressive aids, and you should allow yourself ample opportunity to practice with them. You must discover beforehand what difficulties there may be so that the presentation will go smoothly. Your preparation should include practice to ensure proper timing; the audiovisual aid should appear precisely when it is appropriate and be removed when it has served its purpose. If these guidelines are followed, audiovisual aids can be especially potent forms of support.

Forms of support give the message clarity, impact, and interest. Choosing supporting materials carefully is perhaps the most difficult and

FIGURE 4.2 Audiovisual Aids: Do's and Don't's

Do's

1. Audio and audiovisual aids will seldom be used. When they are used:
   (a) Make sure the audio recording is of good quality and can be easily heard by all members of the audience.
   (b) Make sure the audio aid is synchronized with any accompanying visual aid and with the content of the presentation.
2. Use visual aids to clarify and amplify complex portions of your presentation.
   (a) Graphs, bar charts, and pie charts can clarify raw data by suggesting trends and relationships.
   (b) Photographs can show items too small to be seen by a large audience or too large to visualize.
   (c) Flow charts can illustrate processes.
3. Videotape, films, and filmstrips can be used to illustrate processes, demonstrate complex procedures, provide authoritative support for particular points, and other uses.

Don't's

1. Do not attempt to put too much material on a single visual aid. A good visual aid ought to be easily comprehended at a glance.
2. Do not show a visual aid before the point in the presentation where it complements the speech content; don't leave the visual up longer than necessary.
3. Do not read from visual aids.
4. Do not hand out material to an audience and expect audience members to follow you as you systematically review the material; never ask an audience to pass around materials you provide as you are speaking.

---

important task you face in preparing yourself for public speaking. If you choose carefully, your messages will be both interesting to your audience and effective for you.

The Outline

With all the pieces of the speech now assembled, it is time to show graphically how all the pieces fit together to make a complete message. This is accomplished by preparing an outline. The outline is not prepared for your listeners; it is prepared solely to serve you in several important ways. The outline allows you to see the structural blueprint of the complete message. Each portion of the speech is shown in structural relationship to all other portions, and particular strengths and weaknesses of the message may be made evident. The outline permits you to subject each portion of the speech to careful scrutiny, and flaws which might be difficult to recognize otherwise become easier to spot when graphically displayed. For example, a cursory examination of your main points may reveal that, while your purpose requires them to be treated more or less equally, one main point is very well developed and another is poorly developed. A glance at the number of subpoints supporting each main point in this instance is all that is necessary to identify an area that requires attention. Just as an architect conceives and then commits to detailed blueprints the plan for a new building and then pores over the blueprints to ensure that the building will have structural integrity as well as function and beauty, you must construct and study the speech outline to ensure the effectiveness of your public speeches.

The outline will become a tool to assist you in preparing to deliver the message. In some instances the outline or some truncated version of it will be used during the presentation. In the following chapter, the uses of the outline for practice and presentation will be examined more closely.

Finally, the outline can be a most useful tool for conducting a systematic postanalysis of the speech encounter. The accuracy of your prior situational analysis can be examined by referring to the outline to recall what information or educated guesses guided your choices in putting the message together. As you work through the outline, your adaptive strategies can be compared to listeners' responses during the presentation to reveal the effectiveness of those strategies. Persons who speak frequently in public may retain speech outlines for some time as a record of the speech encounter and as a guide for preparing for similar encounters in the future.

Since the outline is not likely to be seen by the audience, it should be your personal record. While some speech communication textbooks promote specific forms, form should not be allowed to interfere with what you wish to accomplish with the outline. The best form is the one you feel most comfortable with and confident in using. Some guidelines have proved useful and can be recommended; public speaking textbooks[8] consistently recommend the following in preparing outlines: (1) make the major divisions of the speech distinct; (2) use a consistent symbol system to separate ideas; (3) use complete sentences; (4) use only one idea for each symbol system; and (5) be succinct. Let's examine and illustrate each of these guidelines.

The major divisions of the speech include the introduction, the body, and the conclusion. Each division serves distinct functions and so should be distinctly represented in the outline. This can be done in at least two ways. First, each division can be distinctly labeled and treated as a separate unit. For example:

INTRODUCTION

I. Inflation is the greatest threat to America since World War II.
    A. Inflation alone costs Americans $28 billion for each percentage point of increase.
    B. Overpriced goods and services lead directly to reduced consumption and to unemployment.

II. Inflation is the most costly tax we bear.

BODY

I. To defeat inflation we must discover its causes.
    A. Government spending is widely regarded as the most critical cause of inflation.
        1. Deficit spending by government clearly contributes to inflation.
        2. Government spending, however, is not solely responsible for inflation.
    B. Noncompetitive business practices feed inflation.
    C. Abuses of consumer credit contribute to inflation.
    D. Unrealistic wage demands fuel inflation.

II. Inflation can be controlled if we will address its causes.
    A. Government budget deficits must be reduced.
        1. Domestic programs must be made efficient.
        2. Defense spending must be monitored to eliminate waste.
    B. Competition must be restored to the marketplace.
    C. Credit histories must be more closely tied to credit lines.
    D. Unrealistic wage demands must be rejected.

CONCLUSION

I. Inflation is a threat that we recognize and rightly fear.

II. Americans are at their best when they confront a problem, discover its causes, and then apply appropriate solutions.

III. Inflation is the kind of problem that invites us to work together or risk common disaster.

If the major divisions are not treated as separate units the outline looks like this:

I. INTRODUCTION

    A. Inflation is the greatest threat to America since World War II.
        1. Inflation . . .
        2. _____
    B. Inflation is the most costly tax . . .

II.   BODY

    A.   To defeat inflation we must discover its causes
        1.   Government spending . . .
           a.   Deficit spending . . .
           b.   _____
        2.   Noncompetitive business . . .
        3.   _____
        4.   _____
    B.   Inflation can be controlled if we will address its causes
        1.   _____
           a.   _____
           b.   _____
        2.   _____
        3.   _____
        4.   _____

III.   CONCLUSION

    A.   Inflation is a threat . . .
    B.   Americans are at their best . . .
    C.   _____

The difference here may not appear significant, and it isn't in this case. Where the body of the speech contains a number of main points each supported by subpoints, treating each division of the speech as a separate unit will be less cumbersome and graphically less cluttered.

    Notice that in both examples a consistent symbol system is used and coordinate and subordinate relationships among ideas is visually accomplished by indentation. While any consistent symbol system is acceptable, the most common is as follows:

           I.
             A.
                1.
                    a.
                        (1)
                          (a)

In the above examples, the capital letters represent main ideas throughout the speech which are approximately equal in importance (coordinate); the numbers which follow A and B in the second outline clearly indicate supporting or subordinate ideas.

    Since the outline is intended as a comprehensive blueprint to assist prespeech analysis and practice and to facilitate postspeech analysis, complete sentences are recommended. Otherwise you must rely upon memory to remind you of what you intended to say at each point. A cogent phrase may be enough, but a complete sentence is better insurance. If you have never sat at your desk for several awkward minutes attempting to recall what some abstruse phrase on your calendar means, then you are free to ignore this recommendation.

The outline is intended to be a blueprint; you will have to resist the temptation to construct the whole building. Outlines in the hands of inexperienced and somewhat nervous speakers turn into manuscripts. The outline is a graphic representation of the speech and the structural relationships among its various points. It must be as brief as you can manage and yet representative of your plan for achieving your purpose through particular message strategies. You will discover that you can bring a sense of "planned spontaneity" to your presentation if your outline is complete but succinct. Overelaborated outlines surpress spontaneity and complicate several aspects of effective delivery.

Achieving Orality

Good language usage is the stuff of good speeches. But what is good language usage? It is probably much easier for most people to say what is not good language usage. You and I have a sense of what is painful to our ears, but we are hard put to explain precisely what qualities of language stir us and sway us. But it doesn't require much to move from what we easily recognize as poor language usage to what is good language usage. As a public speaker you need to develop an ear for good language usage. And listening to your own words is an effective way to test the quality of the language you expect to use. A brief review of good and bad language habits may assist you to discover how to manage language to serve your purposes.

Good language for public speaking is not consistently complex and technical; rather, it is as clear, direct, and unaffected as we can make it. Chapter 1 argued that an effective public speaker is not someone with a million-dollar vocabulary. If you insist upon parading your newest discoveries from the dictionary before your listeners, you will find them increasingly uninterested or even hostile toward what you have to say. You are well advised to heed Reminder 14 of William Strunk, Jr., and E. B. White:

> Avoid the elaborate, the pretentious, the coy, and the cute. Do not be tempted by a twenty-dollar word when there is a ten-center handy, ready and able. Anglo-Saxon is a livelier tongue than Latin, so use Anglo-Saxon words; in this, as in so many matters pertaining to style, one's ear must be one's guide: *gut* is a lustier noun than *intestine*, but the two words are not interchangeable, because *gut* is often inappropriate, being too coarse for the context. Never call a stomach a tummy without good reason.[9]

Technical terms, repeated use of acronyms, and gobbledygook also complicate public speaking unnecessarily. Technical terms and acronyms are often used unwittingly. Some years ago I struggled with other members of an audience listening to a speaker who sprinkled his presentation with phrases like "cost backlogging on LAM systems," "pre-FARB analogies," and "calculating the degrees of freedom provided by ESS versus leased software." I was quickly lost and so were those around me, even those who were more or less familiar with some of the technical terms being used. Technical terms and especially acronyms are shortcuts for longer and more detailed explanations. They work only if listeners have heard, understood, and can readily recall the detailed explanation. That is a lot of if's upon which to bet the success of your public speaking. You are better advised to assume that your listeners will not understand and will probably be annoyed by technical terms and acronyms unless you have very good information which indicates otherwise.

Gobbledygook, on the other hand, is never justified. Gobbledygook is overblown, pompous, highly abstracted, wordy, and syntactically tortured language frequently associated with government communication but equally rampant in private endeavors. Lawyers, insurance companies, financial institutions, and flimflam artists have—with some notable exceptions—well-deserved reputations for gobbledygook. Note this example from John O'Hayre's instructive and humorous book, *Gobbledygook Has Gotta Go*:

> Area mineral classification will be completed to provide availability of currently valuable mineral resources as well as presently unfavorable mineral occurrences for expanding demands as these occurrences become potentially valuable.[10]

Besides being hopelessly long, this sentence makes no sense. Gobbledygook such as this is tough when it is in print and can be read repeatedly and carefully; when it is spoken, it is impossible. This kind of language abuse is unnecessary. The same idea can be put more simply, more directly, and much more clearly. O'Hayre untangled the sentence to produce this version that was quickly recognized as what was probably meant by the overly modified mess above:

> Mineral classifications will be made by areas; and these will show resources that are available now and those that might become valuable in the future.[11]

A careful reading of O'Hayre's book will help you recognize and avoid oral as well as written gobbledygook.

Good language for public speaking is concrete, conversational, and concise. Words that awaken specific images will attract and interest your listeners. Notice the specificity, the imagery, and the riveting impact of this selection from a speech by Walter B. Wriston, Chairman of the First National City Corporation:

> Government intervention destroys that path to a democratic decision. The result is noneconomic. No one who saw it on television last year will soon forget the wholesale drowning of baby chicks. It was done because the government froze the price on grown chickens at a level which made it uneconomic for farmers to raise and sell them. Government seems loath to learn from experience in tampering with a free market. Drowning chicks was a rerun of the plowing under of surplus cotton and grain and the slaughter of piglets a generation ago.[12]

The movement here from a general indictment of government intervention to the spectre of drowning chicks, slaughtered piglets, and wasted grain is both interesting and effective.

When you use actual names, times, and places in describing real events, you add credibility as well as interest to your speaking. Recall the anecdote used earlier about the note found in a 20-mm shell taken from the fuel tank of a B-17 bomber during World War II. The story is compelling in itself. But what gives it a ring of authenticity and high human drama are the many details it contains. The German fighters fired 20-mm shells. The captain's name was Bohn, and the bomber was called the *Tondelayo*. The note, which was rolled up, was written in Czech. Specificity adds authenticity, interest, and impact. Each time you are tempted to use words and phrases like "some," "very much," "a few," you ought to consider the possibilities of being more specific, more precise—and more credible. As a general rule, you should provide your listeners with as much detail and data as you can manage without becoming tedious.

Being conversational means carrying the qualities of direct person-to-person interaction to public speaking. The best test of the conversational qualities of your speaking may be tested by listening to yourself and asking, "Does that sound like someone talking to another person, or does it sound like someone reading an essay?" Conversational or oral quality generally comes from being succinct. Short sentences are easier for listeners to handle, and simple syntactical constructions aid understanding. As sentences get longer and more complex, listeners must struggle to remember where the sentence started while they wait for it to end. Like jugglers who attempt to juggle a number of objects while constantly catching still more objects, the effort quickly becomes unbearable, and all the objects fall in an incomprehensible heap.

Anglo-Saxon English sentence construction is built around a kernel containing a subject, then a predicate, followed by an object. A kernel looks like this:

John bought a computer.

The more we break up the kernel sentence by inserting words, clauses, and other constructions between the three elements of the kernel sentence, the tougher it is for listeners to follow what we say. Notice how the kernel is complicated by a few routine additions.

John Martin, President of Lyman, Inc., for the past three years, after soliciting and examining bids from twenty-six computer companies,	bought through a combined purchase and lease arrangement which permits Lyman to contract out services to ensure full utilization and three-year amortization of the costs	a 100-megabyte solid-disk, expandable micro-computer system with a printer and overdrive.
↑	↑	↑
JOHN	BOUGHT	A COMPUTER

While it is necessary and appropriate to be complex from time to time, your bias should be toward brevity.

Conversational speech is succint, concrete, detailed, and familiar. There is frequent repetition, restatement, and internal summaries. There is a mixture of the general and specific, and words which suggest personal involvement—words like "I," "you," "we," "ours," and "mine." Finally, conversational speech uses everyday, colloquial language that listeners find familiar and easy to understand. As a general rule, if listeners notice your language usage at all, it is more than likely they will react negatively. Good conversational speech, like good speech organization and good grooming, is most effective when it works without calling attention to itself.

Lest you think conversational speech is synonymous with dull, look what can be done with simple words in the hands of a speaker willing to make the language serve his purposes. Louis Rukeyser, newspaper columnist and host of "Wall Street Week" on Public Service Television, spoke to a business group about how recent presidents had responded to inflation. Lyndon Johnson, he said, "tried to hide the cost of the war in Vietnam," and Richard Nixon "changed his course with every shift in the political winds." So far, this is pretty ordinary stuff; but notice what Rukeyser does with language in discussing the efforts of Gerald Ford and Jimmy Carter to control inflation: "Ford walked stickily and carried a big soft." "Carter continually debated with himself and both sides lost." A turn of phrase and an image suggesting indecision added spice to Rukeyser's speech.[13]

Language is the tool of the effective public speaker. It is a marvelously versatile tool. If you are prepared to make language work for you, you will quickly discover that it is possible to be clear and interesting without resorting to exotic or strained language. To repeat, the effective speaker is not one who has a million-dollar vocabulary and speaks the King's English perfectly. Rather, the effective public speaker is one who speaks plainly and authentically to his or her listeners. In an age when flamboyance in public speaking was the norm, Abraham Lincoln spoke simply, directly, and sincerely. Lincoln was not the featured speaker at Gettysburg, and his simple words were ridiculed by the press. But we don't remember the words of those who shared the platform with him, and we chisel his plain words in rock.

Only one additional word needs to be added to this brief discussion of language usage in public speaking. It should not be necessary, but sad experience suggests the need. I find it unfortunately necessary to caution professional people against the use of vulgar, obscene, racist, and sexist language. Inevitably, some business and professional people succumb to the temptation to tell a racist or sexist joke. Former Agriculture Secretary Earl Butz is but a prominent example of an unfortunately frequent occurrence. Locker-room language has no value in public speeches. Even when you are sure you know the listeners well enough to have a little fun, vulgarity or racist or sexist talk is a bad idea. You cannot predict precisely what will or will not offend even those you believe you know well. And, of course, people talk to people. Your personal credibility as a public person is too valuable to risk on something as worthless, as damaging, and as stupid as vulgarity or racist and sexist talk.

USING SPEECH WRITERS

An assumption of this chapter is that the person who prepares a public message is also the person who will present the speech. Obviously, this is not always the case. Speakers in business, industry, politics and academe often present speeches prepared for them by other people. There is simply not enough time for these busy professionals to prepare adequately all of the messages they are called upon to present. And, of course, they often speak not as individuals but as representatives of complex organizations and institutions. Confronted with such serious responsibility and insufficient time in which to prepare important public messages, professional people often seek help.

While professional people are skilled in many areas, they are not

consistently skilled in the preparation of messages for public presentation. Based upon his outstanding skills in technical and other areas, a
brilliant engineer may rise swiftly to the presidency of a company. But he
may become acutely aware of his deficiencies in preparing important
public messages, especially under the additional handicap of severe time
constraints. That perceptive president will recognize that the fortunes of
his business organization and the livelihoods of his employees depend
upon his effectiveness as the primary spokesperson for his organization.
He wisely seeks help.

This is not an unqualified endorsement of the practice of using
speechwriters. There is something decidedly unsavory about letting
others do your thinking for you or representing as your own what others
have labored to produce. Speech communication scholars and others
have written extensively about and debated heatedly the ethics of ghostwriting.[14] Typically, these arguments conclude with a grudging acknowledgment that ghostwriting is justified under some special circumstances,
but that the individual who employs a ghostwriter has a serious obligation
to monitor critically the prepared messages. Any public speaker must be
prepared to be judged by what he says in public, whether he prepared it
himself or delegated others to prepare it for him.

A brief sketch of the special complexities confronted by the
ghostwriter and the additional obligations faced by those who must use
ghostwriters is appropriate here. Being a ghostwriter is a little like being a
stunt man in a movie. You must work very hard, take some nasty lumps,
and through it all accept the fact that you are effective only if you succeed
in making someone else look and sound good. The effective speech writer
must understand and execute each step in the speech preparation process
except Steps 17, 18, 19 of The Public Presentation Game (see Figure 2.1,
pp. 26–27). The speech writer does everything except rehearse, polish, and
actually present the speech.

Most importantly, the speech writer must examine carefully the
speaker/audience relationship. The message must "fit" the speaker for
whom it is prepared. This means that, insofar as possible, the writer must
faithfully reflect the speaker's attitudes, values, beliefs, and style. And,
since the speaker often speaks for an organization or institution, the
organizational and institutional requirements must be artfully interwoven
into the message. Further, all of this must be creatively adapted to the
particular audience and particular circumstances which the speaker confronts. No simple task.

Recognizing these requirements, the speech writer will seek every
opportunity to know the speaker's attitudes, values, beliefs, prejudices,
habits, and visions of the future. The speaker will become for the ghostwriter the object of intensive and continuing analysis. This may be done
through informal or formal interviews or observations over some period of
time and, if possible, in a number of interactive situations. It is not

surprising that presidential speech writers like Joseph Berger, Theodore Sorensen, Richard Goodwin, and Ray Price were closer than cabinet officers and other advisors to the presidents they served. Sometimes to an uncomfortable degree, speech writers must emulate the speakers they serve.

The speaker who employs a speech writer has similarly serious and complex responsibilities. Interestingly, these responsibilities are similar to other instances in which tasks must be delegated but the responsibility for the outcome remains with the person doing the delegating. The head coach of a professional football team may find it necessary to entrust the offensive game to an assistant coach. But he will be roasted in the sports pages if the offensive team does not play well. A business executive may delegate responsibility for financial planning to a trusted subordinate, but the board of directors and the stockholders will ask for a resignation if the company suffers from poor financial planning. Public communication is a serious, often critically important, activity. The wise professional person will not lightly delegate responsibility for such activity and then ignore the task until it is completed and he or she is handed a tidy manuscript for delivery. I can think of no better formula for courting disasters in public forums than such a cavalier but all too common approach to public speaking.

Between the extremes of preparing all of your own public messages and entrusting the entire task to a speech writer is a procedure which saves time but reduces the risks of using a speech writer. First, during a preliminary meeting with the speech writer, the purpose for speaking, the general topic, the anticipated audience/situation, and other facets of the anticipated encounter can be discussed. Often, it is useful to include in such a meeting individuals whose experience and insights can assist the efforts to prevision the encounter. The speech writer should be encouraged to ask questions of the speaker and the others present and should be allowed to offer suggestions and observations. This first session clearly is an effort to promote a meeting of minds, and dissenting views should be encouraged to avoid "groupthink" or the mere pooling of ignorance. At the conclusion of this meeting the writer should be instructed to prepare an outline of the speech. This initial outline should contain more than is needed for the speech in its final form.

A second meeting, perhaps involving the same people or a well-chosen addition or two, will focus on the outline prepared by the speech writer. Each idea will be examined to determine how well it serves the purpose of the speech, meets the requirements of the anticipated audience/situation, and reflects the character and style of the speaker. The session should not become an opportunity to criticize the speech writer; rather, it should be a cooperative exercise aimed at producing a message well adapted to the speaker, the anticipated audience, and the anticipated circumstances. Ideas may be eliminated, added, expanded, and abbreviated as necessary. The speech writer and the speaker should attempt to frame ideas in language normally used by the speaker. This session should end when all participants are satisfied that the basic structure and content of the message have been identified and framed to meet the audience/situation. The writer should be instructed to prepare a first draft based on the outcome of this session.

In the next session the interaction must be primarily between the speaker and the speech writer. The speaker should examine the draft carefully to see how well it meets the purpose for which it was prepared and how well it reflects the thinking of those who have participated in its creation and development. It is helpful to read the script aloud to hear and feel its rhythm and to test its oral qualities.

Trying on a new speech like this is like trying on a new suit of clothes in a tailor's shop. You want to get the feel of it before you are prepared to agree with the anxious fellow who stands at your elbow assuring you that "It's you." Changing words, phrases, or sentences, moving paragraphs around, adding material and throwing out some—all this is appropriate. People make judgments about your taste—not your tailor's taste—when they look at your clothing. And people judge you and the organization or institution you represent when you present a message in public.

It is sometimes necessary to employ a speech writer to do the bulk of the work in preparing a speech. Given what it takes to do that job well, speech writers should be paid well and treated with respect. Theirs is an unusual and valuable skill. The *Wall Street Journal* recently carried a story describing the search for a speech writer by Chrysler President Lee A. Iacocca. The story indicated that Mr. Iacocca is very demanding, often requiring revisions of speeches at unusual hours and on very short notice. But the article noted that Iacocca was offering up to $90,000 a year for the position. Speech writers should be paid well; but, like Lee Iacocca, speakers should insist on getting their money's worth.

SUMMARY

This chapter began by suggesting that messages are crafted. You begin by generating ideas from which you select the most salient, the most relevant, and the most persuasive. The message then begins to take form as you choose an appropriate organizational format, flesh it out with various forms of support, and build an outline. Working from the outline, you fine tune with language so that you say what you wish to say as effectively as you can manage. Throughout this process it is a good idea to refer to the decisions you make earlier. As you build the message you need to remember your purpose and the information you gleaned from a careful audience/situation analysis. You should ask if all aspects of the message are consistent with your purpose and reflective of the adaptive requirements discovered through your analysis of the audience/situation. And then you should ask if the complete message and its various parts have qualities of compelling interest and vivacity. Listeners expect to be informed, persuaded, or moved to action when they make themselves available to a public speaker. To be a public speaker who is consistently successful, you must move listeners to embrace your purposes eagerly—even enthusiastically. Some speeches succeed because the need is evident and the speaker manages to do what is required without making any serious mistakes. But the speaker who seizes the opportunity to accomplish what is needed and does so with enthusiasm and flair is the speaker who is consistently successful and richly deserves such success.

Finally, this chapter considered the vexing matter of speech writers: when and why they should be used, and the special complexities and ethics faced by both speech writers and those for whom they write.

Notes

1. Wilson, J. F., and Arnold, C. C., *Public Speaking as a Liberal Art*, 3rd ed. (Boston: Allyn and Bacon, 1974), 165.

2. For examples of the application of the Monroe Motivated Sequence to particular situations, see Ehninger, D., Monroe, A. H., and Gronbeck, B., *Principles and Types of Speech Communication*, 9th ed. (Glenview, Ill: Scott, Foresman, 1982).

3. Winans, J. A., *Public Speaking* (New York: Century, 1917).

4. For representative studies of initial source credibility, see Andersen, K. E., "An Experimental Study of the Interaction of Artistic and Non-Artistic Ethos in Persuasion" (Ph.D. diss., University of Wisconsin, 1961); Brooks, R., and Scheidel, T., "Speech as Process: A Case Study," *Speech Monographs*, 1968, no. 35:1–7; Andersen, K. E., and Clevenger, T., Jr., "A Summary of Experimental Research in Ethos," *Speech Monographs*, 1963, no. 30:58–78.

5. Bendiner, E., *The Fall of Fortresses* (New York: G. P. Putnam's Sons, 1980).

6. Morris, E., *The Rise of Theodore Roosevelt* (New York: Coward, McCann, and Geoghegan, 1979), 470.

7. Bitzer, L. F., "The Rhetorical Situation," *Philosophy and Rhetoric*, 1968, no. 1:6.

8. See, for example, Wilson, J. F., and Arnold, C. C., *Public Speaking as a Liberal Art*, 3rd ed. (Boston: Allyn and Bacon, Inc., 1974), 192–208; Devito, J. A., *The Elements of Public Speaking* (New York: Harper & Row, 1976), 205–13; and Osborn, M., *Speaking in Public* (Boston: Houghton Mifflin, 1980), 218–34.

9. Strunk, W., Jr., and White, E. B., *The Elements of Style*, 3rd ed. (New York: Macmillan, 1979), 76–77.

10. O'Hayre, J., *Gobbledygook Has Gotta Go* (Washington, D.C.: U.S. Government Printing Office, 1966), 30. (0-206-141).

11. O'Hayre, 31.

12. Wriston, W. B., "The Whale Oil, Chicken, and Energy Syndrome." An address before the Economic Club of Detroit, February 25, 1974, p. 6. Distributed by the Publications Unit, First National City Bank, 18th Floor, 399 Park Avenue, New York 10022.

13. Rukeyser, L., Speech at the Pabst Theater, October 5, 1982, as reported by The *Milwaukee Sentinel*, October 6, 1982, Part 2, 6.

14. Discussions of the ethics of ghostwriting and the methods of ghostwriting are plentiful. Representative pieces include: Golden, J. L., "John F. Kennedy and the 'Ghosts,'" *Quarterly Journal of Speech*, 1966, no. 52:348–57; Hall, R., N., "Lyndon Johnson's Speech Preparation," *Quarterly Journal of Speech*, 1965, no. 51:168–76; Benson, T. W., "Conversations with a Ghost," *Today's Speech*, 1968, no. 16:71–81.

CHAPTER 5

Practicing and Presenting the Public Speech: Mastering Delivery

This chapter is about delivery. Listeners will often excuse defects in delivery if the message is compelling. Because the content of the speeches was vital to some interest of ours, you and I have sat through any number of badly delivered speeches. But we dare not rely repeatedly upon the intrinsic interest of listeners in what we have to say; audience toleration of delivery deficiency cannot—and should not—be counted on. Superbly prepared speeches can fail because of poor delivery, and mediocre messages do sometimes get transformed into rousing successes by good delivery. Mastering speech delivery is a matter, then, of gaining an edge, an edge which may spell the difference between success and failure.

Therefore, while speech delivery is not a first consideration in preparing yourself for public communication, it is an important consideration worthy of careful thought and preparation. If you have good reason to speak, if you have analyzed the audience/situation, and if you have carefully crafted a well-adapted message, then attention to delivery is appropriate.

What is good delivery? Part of the answer is that delivery, like the message elements discussed in the previous chapter, is adapted to the audience/situation. Good vocal qualities, movements, gestures, and facial expressions reinforce and complement your words. Such delivery is likely to feel natural to you and appear to be unremarkable to your audience. If delivery calls attention to itself, it is probably poorly adapted and may well be perceived as phony. Good delivery helps you accomplish your purpose by conveying your message completely, clearly, and with precisely calibrated emotional intensity—not too little and not too much. Good delivery is delivery that enables you to establish and maintain an image of yourself as a competent, confident public speaker. Good delivery suggests to listeners that you have prepared carefully, that you are in control of yourself and your message, and that you are interested in their responses. Good delivery, perhaps more than anything else you do in preparing yourself for public speaking, will determine if you are perceived as a competent public person, or if you are perceived as an unfortunate soul called upon to do what you do not do well.

METHODS OF PREPARATION

A first decision in preparing yourself for effective delivery is the selection of a method of presentation. Among the choices are memorization, manuscript speaking, and extemporaneous presentation. Unless you are blessed with instant recall and the skill of a professional actor to make the printed word sound conversational without extensive practice, memorization is an inappropriate choice. Manuscript speaking is appropriate for some kinds of speaking situations, but there are inherent hazards in this method. I will discuss the circumstances that justify the use of a manuscript, and I will offer a method of manuscript delivery which will assist you to overcome the hazards of manuscript delivery while retaining its advantages. Primary emphasis, however, will be upon extemporaneous delivery, because it will most appropriately fit the majority of the speaking situations you will confront.

Extemporaneous Speaking

Extemporaneous speaking is carefully prepared but designed to permit spontaneity. If this sounds like a contradiction, it is not. When you speak extemporaneously, you speak with a preidentified speech structure and a clear idea about what kinds of supporting materials you will use throughout the speech. You do not, however, know precisely what you will say. To prepare for extemporaneous delivery, you prepare a complete outline, practice from the outline, and then rely during the presentation upon a few notes on a few note cards. Your practice would assure that you know what you want to say and in what order, but you retain sufficient flexibility to expand upon particular points, to clarify ideas that appear to be difficult for your listeners, or to make other adjustments that the audience/situation appears to require as it unfolds before you.

The hallmark of extemporaneous delivery is flexibility. If your preparation for extemporaneous delivery has been thorough you should be able to speak with almost continuous eye contact with your listeners. Extemporaneous delivery allows you to monitor listeners continuously for feedback. Additionally, because you need only refer to a few notes, you have freedom to move and gesture freely and naturally. Your speaking appears spontaneous, conversational, and genuine.

It is a mistake, however, to assume that extemporaneous delivery is easier or less time-consuming than other presentational formats. Certainly you are not required to write out the speech word for word, but you must take the time to know the speech structure very thoroughly, to know what to say and generally how you want to say it. And you must practice sufficiently to ensure that all points are covered adequately while a sense of conversational spontaneity is preserved. This is no mean trick. Even experienced, professional speakers will devote considerable preparation time to ensure that extemporaneous speeches are delivered with fluency as well as flexibility.

Extemporaneous speaking is appropriate for most speaking situations, but there are limitations. Obviously, extemporaneous speaking is not appropriate when the speaking situation requires precise timing and precise language. If you are permitted exactly fifteen minutes to speak to a radio or television audience, or if you are permitted a ten-minute segment of a telephone conference session made available to a business group, extemporaneous speaking would be clearly inappropriate. Formal occasions often require formal presentations. In Chapter 1 I referred to a speech by Robert V. Krikorian—the annual Peter E. Rentscher Memorial Lecture. Without question this was a formal occasion. Careful preparation, including the use of a manuscript, was appropriate. The lecture is reprinted and widely circulated, and the speaker is expected to provide a verbatim copy of the lecture. On other occasions precision in wording is critical. You may recall the speech given by President Kennedy during the Cuban missile crisis in 1962. President Kennedy was rightly concerned that a misspoken word or phrase could produce a misunderstanding that would provoke a major war between the United States and the Soviet Union. That was not a time to rely upon extemporaneous speech. Increasingly, business and professional people are confronted with speaking situations that include representatives of the print and electronic media. A precise record of what was said—and what was not said—is often essential. Extemporaneous delivery does not meet this requirement.

Extemporaneous delivery is not particularly fluent unless it is well rehearsed. It is likely to include a number of "uh's" and "ah's" and other fillers as the speaker gropes for a particular word or phrase. Unless you have made yourself very familiar with the structure of the speech you are apt to forget portions of the speech, especially if you depart from the preplanned speech structure to respond to some contingency that emerges from the audience/situation. Such departures from what was planned often result in confusion or difficulty in getting back to the speech structure. While extemporaneous delivery is appropriate for most of the speaking situations you will confront, it should not be taken lightly. Extemporaneous delivery demands careful preparation and conscientious practice. A bit later in this chapter I will offer suggestions for practicing the extemporaneous speech.

Manuscript Speaking

Delivering a speech from a manuscript offers a number of advantages. You have the opportunity to control time very precisely and to choose your words to ensure maximum understanding and impact. The manuscript is a tangible record of the speaking encounter and may be used, if necessary, to correct the public record. If it is handled properly, the manuscript speech is devoid of most of the nonfluencies found in conversational speech. Because it is prepared to be delivered verbatim, the manuscript speech can be reviewed by a number of people who can point out potential hazards and offer suggestions to make it more effective. Speech writers are seldom used to prepare speeches for extemporaneous delivery; they are typically employed to prepare or assist in the preparation of manuscript speeches. Like other speakers, you may find it reassuring to speak with a manuscript in front of you—no need to worry about forgetting or misspeaking during the presentation. What you want to say is right there in front of you; all you need do is read it.

The disadvantages of the manuscript presentation are apparent. Because it is read, it sounds like reading. Most speakers do not read aloud well. Speeches read from manuscript take on a mechanical quality that is easily recognized by listeners. And because you must look at the manuscript while reading from it, you lose direct eye contact with listeners and the sense of direct communication that is appropriate and necessary for effective oral communication; and of course if you do not look at your listeners, you cannot monitor their responses or feedback to what you are saying. Finally, speeches read from manuscript inevitably are read at a rate that is too rapid for effective communication. You read much faster than you speak, and it is difficult to restrain the tendency to read aloud at a reading rate rather than a slower, more comprehensible and interesting speaking rate. Reading the manuscript typically produces a more rapid rate that is flat and unvaried; the normal pauses that accompany conversational speech are abbreviated or ignored altogether. The result too often is a speech that sounds like an essay on legs, presented by a speaker eager to finish an unsavory and painful task. Listeners, unfortunately, must share the pain; they, too, are usually happy when such awkward interactions end.

The potential dangers of manuscript speaking ought to make you cautious in deciding whether or not to use a manuscript, but potential abuse ought not prevent appropriate use. As noted earlier, manuscript presentations are necessary and appropriate under circumstances where precision in language and time management are critical. In response to the legitimate needs for manuscript speaking, and in view of the potential hazards such presentations pose, I have developed a format which I have tested and taught to scores of business and professional people. The format, which I call the *quarter-sheet manuscript format*, has proved helpful to those who have used it.

The Quarter-Sheet Manuscript Format

A sample page illustrating the quarter-sheet manuscript format is provided in Figure 5.1. (p. 100). Study the page for a moment: several of its features may be obvious. First, all of the script is shifted to the upper-right corner of the page. You and I read from left to right, and what is on the right side of the page seems to be easier to see quickly. Second, when you stand at a lectern reading from a manuscript, your head and eyes typically drop as you move down the page. That drop becomes more pronounced as your eyes move past an area near the middle of the page. I refer to the area as the mid-page zone. Putting the script in the upper-right corner of the page makes it easier for most people to see and reduces the extent to which the head drops when reading from the manuscript. Consequently, it is easier for most people to look from the manuscript toward the listeners and back to the manuscript. Your eyes are always close to the listeners as well as the script.

The script is typed in Orator or Statesman type, available on IBM typewriters. This type has been specifically developed to facilitate oral reading from a manuscript. You may find suitable substitutes on other typewriters and word-processing machines. In a pinch, you can type the script in capital letters. Script typefaces are not recommended; they are difficult to read in manuscripts.

All script is typed with no indentations on the left margin to indicate paragraphs or major divisions. Oral presentations require you to pause for varying lengths of time to indicate major and minor thought divisions. Indentations are unsuitable because they are uniform. Pauses of varied length are better indicated visually by extra lines of spacing. Notice in the example that there is an extra line of spacing between two ideas that are apparently part of a series. Two, three, four, or more extra lines of spacing can be used to indicate visually the separation of ideas.

Sentences are not permitted to intrude past the mid-page line. No sentence is carried over to the next page. And there are no hyphenations at the right margin; in oral presentations, a hyphenation may produce an awkward pronunciation or mispronunciation, and fluency may be adversely affected by carrying a sentence over to the next page.

The transition from one page to another is facilitated in the quarter-

FIGURE 5.1 The Quarter-Sheet Format Page

IF YOU AS BUSINESS PEOPLE DO NOT ACCEPT THE CHALLENGE TO BE EFFECTIVE PUBLIC PERSONS, THEN CONTINUED POOR COMMUNICATION WILL BREED STILL GREATER PUBLIC DISTRUST OF BUSINESS. CAN YOU AFFORD THAT? I THINK NOT!

YOU NEED TO BE EFFECTIVE PUBLIC PERSONS, TOO, FOR YOUR OWN PERSONAL AND PROFESSIONAL DEVELOPMENT. CARL SAGAN, IN HIS BOOK, BROCA'S BRAIN, ARGUES THAT THE DEVELOPMENT OF HUMAN THOUGHT AND INDUSTRY GOES HAND IN HAND WITH THE DEVELOPMENT OF ARTICULATE SPEECH.

(Richard Sennett in . . .)

sheet format in three ways. Since a slight pause naturally occurs at the end of each thought, and since no sentence or thought unit is carried over to the next page, the naturally occurring pause at the end of the last sentence on the page can be used to move to the next page without interrupting the fluency of the talk. Typically, you would simply slide the completed page to one side to reveal the next page. This can be done easily and unobtrusively at the end of the last sentence of each page. Also, the first three or four words of the next page are included on the page just below the script in parenthesis and against the right margin. Your eyes can quickly scan these words to facilitate further the smooth and un-noticeable movement to each new page. Further, the first three or four words of each page are underlined to help guide the eyes quickly to the script. You will soon discover what works best for you as you experiment with various methods to ensure an easy transition to each page.

Occasionally it is helpful to introduce extemporaneous elements into manuscript presentations. In lengthy, formal presentations the audience may welcome a change of pace and tone. In addition, speakers may wish to achieve more direct contact with the audience. This may be especially important when the speaker is offering a personal commitment, reassurance, or personal information (see Figure 5.2, p. 102).

All that is required is that the material to be delivered extemporaneously be identified and practiced so it can be delivered fluently and effectively. Then the normal quarter-sheet format can be interrupted by a page that makes a suitably cryptic reference to the extemporaneous material to be used.

Audiovisuals and the Quarter-Sheet Format

The quarter-sheet manuscript format may also be readily adapted to presentations using audiovisuals. All that is required is that the audio or visual aid be integrated within the manuscript text. This can be done simply by placing an easily seen dot at the point in the text when the audio or visual aid should be utilized. The left column can be used to indicate the nature of the audio or visual aid.

This format provides two distinct advantages: First, the aid can be introduced at precisely the appropriate time. Too many presentations routinely introduce visual aids at the beginning of a sentence or at the beginning of a major point in the presentation. This often produces an awkward moment while audience members react to the visual aid and wait for the explanation of its significance. A smoother, more effective presentation results if aids are introduced at the moment they are needed. In addition, this format allows the speaker to handle audiovisual aids easily and without distraction. There is no need, for example, to check the screen to determine if the correct slide is showing. With practice, slides

FIGURE 5.2 Extemporaneous Material Incorporated in the Quarter-Sheet Format

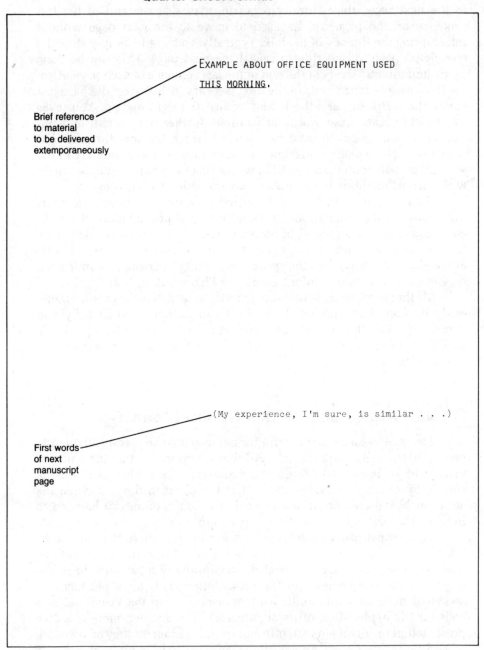

FIGURE 5.3   Audiovisuals Incorporated in the Quarter-Sheet Format

●

bar graph showing five
year raw sales figures

●

graph showing profit
increases over past
five years

QUARTERLY FIGURES ● SHOW A STEADY INCREASE
IN SALES OVER THE PAST FIVE YEARS. THERE IS
NO QUESTION THAT OUR MARKETING, DISTRIBUTION,
AND SALES DEPARTMENTS HAVE DONE AN OUTSTAND-
ING JOB.

BUT MORE ENCOURAGING STILL ARE THE FIGURES
SHOWING THE PROFIT ● FOR THE COMPANY OVER
THE SAME PERIOD. AS YOU CAN SEE, OUR PROFITS
HAVE INCREASED STEADILY AS WE ACHIEVED COST
SAVINGS IN OUR MANUFACTURING PROCESSES.
THAT'S TEAMWORK . . . AND THAT'S WHAT THIS
COMPANY IS ALL ABOUT!

(The combination of efficiency . . .)

can be projected onto the screen using a remote switch without the speaker looking at the screen. The slides appear like magic precisely when they are needed, while the speaker maintains eye contact with the listeners, monitoring audience reactions to the speaker's words as well as the visual aid.

Note the sample format sheet in Figure 5.3 (p. 103). A pencil eraser and an ink pad are all that is necessary to provide the dots. Practice with the format will result in smooth handling of audiovisual aids.

As you might guess, there are apt to be a sizable number of pages used with the quarter-sheet format. Paper is relatively cheap; better to use a little more of it than risk struggling through a manuscript which presents a number of visual obstacles. Pagination is included in the upper-left corner of the page, so that the pages can be organized before and after the presentation. It should not be necessary to refer to the pagination during the presentation.

A scheme indicating the features of the quarter-sheet format is provided in Figure 5.4. I have found it useful to provide such an outline to the typist who prepares the speech manuscript. Later in this chapter I give suggestions for practicing the presentation using the quarter-sheet manuscript format. Before doing that, however, I want to briefly review critical elements in effective delivery.

EFFECTIVE DELIVERY

In order to master the technique of effective delivery in a public speaking situation, there are five elements in which you must become proficient. They are: (1) eye contact; (2) good posture; (3) use of body language; (4) using your voice properly; and (5) practicing your delivery.

Eye Contact

Perhaps the most critical element in effective delivery of public speeches is eye contact. Your ability to look at your audience while you speak to them will determine whether or not they see you as credible. This should not be surprising. We expect people to look at us when they speak to us, and we are puzzled and sometimes annoyed when people—including public speakers—do not look at us when they speak. Moreover, we expect to have good eye contact. When you use good eye contact, you look at the eyes of your listeners and engage their attention and interest. The length of time required to do this varies. You would not, of course, stare at any one listener for an extended period of time, and you would not shift your eyes quickly from listener to listener or sweep the audience

FIGURE 5.4 *Features of the Quarter-Sheet Format*

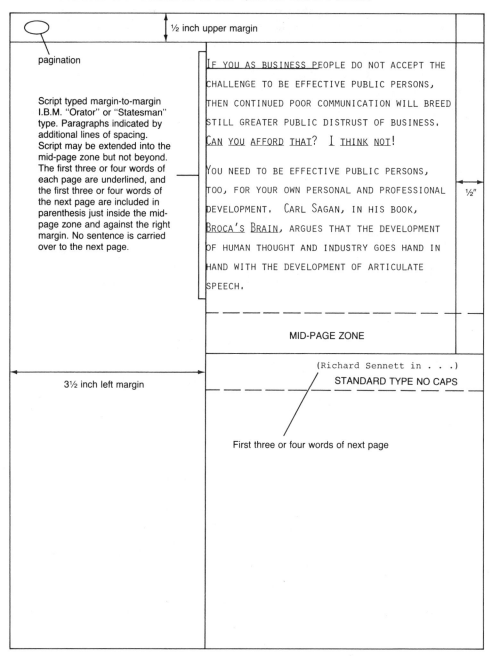

½ inch upper margin

pagination

Script typed margin-to-margin I.B.M. "Orator" or "Statesman" type. Paragraphs indicated by additional lines of spacing. Script may be extended into the mid-page zone but not beyond. The first three or four words of each page are underlined, and the first three or four words of the next page are included in parenthesis just inside the mid-page zone and against the right margin. No sentence is carried over to the next page.

IF YOU AS BUSINESS PEOPLE DO NOT ACCEPT THE CHALLENGE TO BE EFFECTIVE PUBLIC PERSONS, THEN CONTINUED POOR COMMUNICATION WILL BREED STILL GREATER PUBLIC DISTRUST OF BUSINESS. CAN YOU AFFORD THAT? I THINK NOT!

YOU NEED TO BE EFFECTIVE PUBLIC PERSONS, TOO, FOR YOUR OWN PERSONAL AND PROFESSIONAL DEVELOPMENT. CARL SAGAN, IN HIS BOOK, BROCA'S BRAIN, ARGUES THAT THE DEVELOPMENT OF HUMAN THOUGHT AND INDUSTRY GOES HAND IN HAND WITH THE DEVELOPMENT OF ARTICULATE SPEECH.

½"

MID-PAGE ZONE

(Richard Sennett in . . .)
STANDARD TYPE NO CAPS

3½ inch left margin

First three or four words of next page

with your eyes in the manner of a drugstore surveillance camera. Good eye contact is not mechanical; rather, it attempts to carry the sense of direct person-to-person interaction to public encounters.

Good eye contact is often a matter of appropriate timing. Both extemporaneous speaking and speaking from a manuscript require you to look at your notes or the manuscript from time to time. Audience members regard such occasional interruptions as normal; they may view them as indications of your preparation for speaking. But frequent and erratic interruptions of eye contact or interruptions of eye contact at critical moments are apt to be noticed and judged negatively. Frequent and erratic interruptions of eye contact can be detrimental to your credibility as a speaker.

There are, of course, times when direct, continuous eye contact is critical. For example, since listeners make important judgments about your credibility in the first few moments of the speech, direct and continuous eye contact for the first few minutes of the speech is vitally important. A first task in the beginning of the speech is to attract the attention of the listeners. That is very difficult to do if your attention is focused on notes, the lectern, or the floor. When you make a personal commitment to the listeners, when you ask listeners to make a commitment to you or your ideas, or when you issue a challenge, these are occasions when direct, sustained eye contact is critical. As you become more experienced as a public communicator you will learn to discover other points in public speeches where your judgment suggests you will be more effective if you look at your audience. And of course you must look at your audience to note responses to your ideas. If your eyes are glued to notes or a manuscript you will miss the responses which indicate how well you are doing at those critical points where your overall success in speaking is often decided.

Posture

Posture is an aspect of delivery often ignored or lightly regarded. There is not much to say about posture. Good posture simply means standing up straight with your shoulders parallel to the floor. You should look relaxed but alert. Posture becomes a problem when speakers get a little lazy. Slumping to one side or the other, standing on one foot, or draping the upper body over a lectern are common problems with posture. Usually all that is necessary to correct such bad habits is a little attentiveness. Poor posture is not likely to be the cause of failure in public speaking; it is, compared with other aspects of preparation and delivery, a minor matter. But success in public speaking is often determined by how such "minor" matters are managed.

Body Language

Gestures and movement and facial expression are typically exaggerated concerns for public speakers. Public speakers—especially inexperienced public speakers—spend far too much time worrying about what to do with their hands, arms, and body. Should I gesture at this point? Should I smile or frown at different points? Should I move to my right or left, forward or back? Such questions have no answers because they are inappropriate. They deflect attention from what is really important in managing what is often referred to as "body language" in public speaking.

You are apt to manage body language effectively if you focus on some common-sense principles. Gestures, facial expressions, and movement are intended to complement what you are saying. In conversation we move, gesture, and change facial expressions easily and naturally. In public speaking we need to emulate the naturalness of conversation. As a public speaker you are expected to show levels of animation, commitment, and emotional intensity consistent with the content and purpose of your speech. This is done in large measure through gestures, movement, and facial expressions.

Managing body language is not a matter of putting on a proper face or orchestrating the right gestures and correct movements at just the right moment. In fact, most attempts at such contrived body language suffer because they look contrived. For years professional comedians have garnered sure-fire laughs with routines aping the ill-timed, exaggerated or overly timed, and clearly preplanned gestures, facial expressions, and movements of public speakers. Spontaneity and genuineness are the hallmarks of effective body language.

Achieving spontaneity and naturalness in body language is primarily a matter of overcoming bad habits. To gesture, move, and change facial expressions easily requires you to remove restraints that inhibit spontaneity. The body must be freed to do what comes naturally. For example, it is very difficult to move meaningfully if you insist upon standing behind a lectern. Gestures are difficult if you continually grip a lectern or lock your hands and arms behind your back or stick one or both hands in your pockets. If, on the other hand, you stand in a relaxed but alert posture with your arms dropped comfortably to your sides, your hands and arms are free to gesture, and you are free to move. All that remains is for you to focus intently on the sense of urgency and importance that brought you to speak publicly.

Several simple rules follow from this approach to managing body language. They may be summarized as follows:

1. Don't use preplanned gestures, movements, or facial ex-

pressions. Contrived body language almost inevitably looks contrived, and consequently communicates a discrepant message to your audience.

2. Free your body to move and gesture in response to your speech content and the interactive situation. Stand erect but comfortably with your arms at your sides. If your hands and arms are in an awkward position, simply drop them to your sides and focus on what you are trying to say to your listeners. Your hands and arms are not likely to stay at your sides for very long—even though that is a perfectly acceptable pose for public speaking.

3. Don't feel obligated to engage constantly in gesturing and movement. Body language must complement what is said in public speaking; it defeats that purpose when it begins to call attention to itself. I have seen effective public speeches delivered by speakers who did not move at all and gestured very little.

4. Make your gestures, movements, and facial expressions fit the particular speaking situation. It's a mistake to expect to make a subtle point with a slight change in your facial expression if you are speaking to a large audience. They won't see the facial expression, and they'll miss the point. Gestures, movements, and facial expressions have to be broader or more restrained depending upon the size of the audience, the setting, and the subject matter.

5. Work to eliminate extraneous and distracting body language. Some years ago I was told by a speech teacher that I had a habit of stamping my right foot at strange points in public speeches. I wasn't emphasizing anything; I was simply displaying a nervous habit that confused my audiences. Foot stamping, constant hand chopping, pacing, leg swinging, and hand movements around the eyes and mouth are common, distracting habits that can be eliminated by a little attentiveness and an intense focus on what you are trying to achieve with an audience through public talk.

Voice

Your voice is a marvelous instrument; properly used it can inspire, convince, clarify, and stimulate your listeners. Poor vocal quality can ruin an otherwise effective presentation. I believe almost everyone is capable of developing effective vocal delivery for public speaking. I have encountered weak voices, nasal-sounding voices, overly loud voices, and voices that were monotonous. I have never encountered a voice that could not be improved both for public speaking and as a result of public speaking. Effective vocal delivery is varied and well adapted to the speaking situation. For example, your voice must be heard to be effective, but it should not be continuously loud. Volume typically goes up when you are emphasizing a point or when you are conveying intense emotion. It should never drop below the level necessary for it to be heard by all members of your audience. You must be heard, but you need not shout continuously.

The pitch of your voice results from the rate at which your vocal folds vibrate. If the vocal folds vibrate rapidly, a high pitch is produced; if they vibrate slowly, a low pitch results. Because men usually have vocal cords that are thicker and longer than women's, they have voices with lower pitches. Shorter and thinner vocal folds produce higher pitch. Strong emotional intensity produces high pitch as tension causes the vocal folds to vibrate more rapidly. As you relax, pitch levels drop. The trick is to make the pitch of your voice appropriately reflective of the feeling you are trying to convey. Public speeches rarely begin and end with high emotional intensity. Emotion and intensity usually build gradually toward a climax and then descend as the speech ends. Occasionally, a speech will end on a note of intensity and urgency. Such variations in feeling are accomplished by adjusting the pitch and volume accordingly.

Your speaking rate is perhaps the most easily controllable aspect of your vocal delivery. Speaking rapidly suggests intensity and excitement, while speaking slowly suggests deliberation, thoughtfulness, or even sinister intent. Most people in public speaking situations speak too rapidly. They habitually speak at a reading rate or at a rate closer to the rate at which they think. Your rate should ensure intelligibility and ample opportunities for your listeners to assimilate what you say. At the same time, your rate should not be entirely predictable. Variations in rate, like variations in volume and pitch, allow you to be precise in your efforts to convey meaning to your audience. And such vocal variety will attract and hold the interest of the audience. Indeed, what has been detailed in this discussion of volume, pitch, and rate is nothing more than a brief analysis of what usually happens when people speak to each other about things they consider to be important.

Improving your voice can be accomplished with practice and persistence. To improve volume and pitch, try placing a tape recorder at the far end of a large room. Set the microphone level on the tape recorder at a normal range. Then speak from the other end of the room. Imagine your sound waves moving across the room and rolling gently down the far wall. Vary the volume and pitch to convey various emotions: to emphasize, to provoke reflection, to suggest humor. Listen to your voice, and make the adjustments you feel are necessary to achieve precision in meaning and to ensure attention and interest. Be particularly alert to the need to be understood with every syllable, every word, and every idea. Such practice ought to be undertaken in a spirit of thoughtful experimentation. The human voice—your voice—can be remarkably effective in communicating ideas and emotions. It is capable of unlimited variation in conveying the gamut of human emotion. You need only to discover for yourself what you can do with your voice when you try; then you need only do what you know you can.

Practice

Good delivery results from good practice. You need to discover how long you need to practice to be effective, and you need to develop good practice habits. We all seem to know intuitively how long we should prepare to do well. Whether it's studying for a test, preparing an important report, or getting ready to speak in public, we have a pretty good idea of when we are ready and when we are not. It's almost as if there is a small voice in the back of our heads that assures us we are as ready as we can be or warns us we have not done all we can to prepare thoroughly. That small voice whispers a different message for each individual, because individuals differ greatly in how they prepare themselves. Your task is to discover what it takes to be truly prepared. As you become more experienced as a public speaker, you will discover ways to become more efficient and more effective in speech delivery. How often should you practice and how long should you continue your practice? You must answer both questions for yourself.

I can offer suggestions that have worked for me and those I have instructed for fifteen years:

1. Regular practice is preferable to lengthy cram sessions. If you had only twelve hours to practice the delivery of your speech, it would be better to practice twice a day for an hour each session over a six-day period than to practice six hours a day for two days or to cram all your practice into one marathon 12-hour session. Practicing for public speaking, like other worthy pursuits, benefits from regular intervals that permit you to assimilate and integrate what you have learned from one session to the next. Cram sessions, on the other hand, often extend past the point of diminishing returns; you are working very hard but achieving very little.

2. Practice is best done when you are rested. Professional people attempt practice for public speeches too often when they are tired. Practice sessions are a vexing chore under such circumstances. I have recommended many times that professional people set aside some time when energy levels are up to par for productive and efficient practice. Many business people are morning people; they like to get up early and get a head start on the day. I recommend they use a portion of that morning time to practice for speaking. Let someone else walk the dog. A short session after dinner or later in the evening after you have had an opportunity to unwind a bit from the day's activities is also worth it.

3. Establish and follow a practice plan so that each session achieves maximum results. Before you begin to practice the delivery of your speech, you should map out a tentative agenda for each anticipated practice session, focusing on specific objectives for each session. Then after each session, spend a moment or two to make necessary adjustments and to establish the agenda for the next session. As with any task you expect to do thoroughly and well, a little organization at the beginning pays dividends in the efficiency and effectiveness with which the task is completed.

4. Practice under circumstances that offer the fewest distractions. You can't practice effectively in an office with telephones ringing and associates seeking you out for consultation. You can't practice on an airplane, and you can't practice in the den with the television set tuned to a football game. Find a place and a time conducive to good concentration. Basement recreation rooms receive my vote.

5. Make your practice sessions as realistic as possible. Your practice sessions should simulate as closely as possible the anticipated speaking circumstances. For example, *always practice aloud.* Get to know the sound of the speech and the feel of its rhythm as well as its content. Don't whisper! If possible, have others sit in the back of the room to assure that your voice will reach all corners of the room. If possible, practice in the room to be used or a room as similar as you can manage. If you expect to use a lectern, practice with a lectern. If you plan to use audio or visual aids, practice with them so they can be handled easily and efficiently.

6. Don't practice in front of a mirror! I have never seen a public speech delivered with the speaker looking into a mirror. Part of what you are attempting to achieve is a focus on what you are saying and how listeners are responding to you and to your message. A mirror focuses you on you. You see all your physical flaws and indications of nervous self-consciousness. If you are interested in eliminating certain bad habits or want reaction to what you are doing, invite an interested listener or two or use a videocamera to record the speech for subsequent analysis. An audio-recorder can help you monitor the sound of what you do. In using such equipment, remember to view the encounter as potential audience members will. They won't be concerned about the piece of lint on your left sleeve; they're more interested in overall effects. Be as objective as you can be; make each practice session a rehearsal for the anticipated event.

7. Time your presentation as you practice to assure yourself that you are meeting the requirements of the audience/situation. If necessary, add or delete material to achieve proper use of time. Do not attempt to use your speaking rate as the primary means of meeting time constraints. A noticeably rapid speaking rate or a ploddingly slow rate will reduce your effectiveness.

8. Use the practice session to rephrase the speech, to make minor structural changes, to test supporting materials, and to refine your delivery. Good public speeches are constantly being fine tuned, massaged, and calibrated. If your practice sessions represent for you opportunities to improve all aspects of your preparation, then practice will serve you well. If, however, your practice sessions are merely efforts to engrain through repetition the results of preliminary thinking and planning, you may anticipate poor results.

Practice sessions for extemporaneous delivery will differ from those for presentations using the quarter-sheet manuscript format. For example, the extemporaneous presentation will usually require that you begin practice sessions using a fairly complete outline. Over a series of practice sessions, you should be able to abbreviate the outline and eventually come to rely only on a few easily read lines on a note card.

Your goals in practicing for extemporaneous presentations should be to gain complete command of the structure of the speech so that you know what you have done and what is left to be done throughout your presentation. You must retain a sense of spontaneity and flexibility. You will never practice the presentation using the same words twice. If you know the structure of the speech very well, and if you know how you wish to state the ideas in the speech, you will retain spontaneity and possess the flexibility to make some alterations in the presentation as the situation and the responses of the audience require.

Each practice session should include two or more complete run-throughs. Speak aloud and do not start over once you've begun. Despite mistakes, slips, and forgotten ideas, begin at the beginning and continue to the end. If you are to achieve fluency and continuity in delivery, you must discipline yourself. In actual presentations, speakers who start, stop, apologize, and start over mark themselves as poorly prepared and inexperienced public speakers. You may falter a bit, but even experienced speakers falter. Experienced speakers recover and continue like well-trained athletes whose errors only illuminate their skills. When you are confident that you can move smoothly from beginning to end with fluency, smoothness, spontaneity, and a keen sense of direct communication, quit. At this point that voice in the back of your head should be congratulating you on the thoroughness of your preparation. If you're not confident, of course, continue to practice.

Practicing for a presentation using the quarter-sheet manuscript format is a bit more complicated because there are three major tasks to be accomplished. First, you must give a dynamic and appropriate oral interpretation of the manuscript. Even though the speech is written word-for-word, you must imbue the script with the spirit of direct, conversational speech. Second, you must achieve a smooth, fluent delivery. Your mastery of the manuscript format should be so complete that the audience will easily overlook the fact that you are using a manuscript. They should not see you moving pages, and there should be no vocal pauses attributable to the layout of the manuscript. Finally, you must use the quarter-sheet manuscript format to its maximum visual advantage so that your eye contact with the audience is approximately 80 percent of your delivery time. And the eye contact should be meaningful; that is, eye contact should occur at points where it is expected and particularly effective in reinforcing the ideas contained in the speech. The following practice suggestions focus on each of these tasks in turn.

To achieve a dynamic and appropriate oral interpretation of the talk, spend some time reviewing the purpose and structure of the talk. (If the talk has been prepared for you, "reviewing" should be read as "discovering," and considerable time should be devoted to this first task.) Review the meaning of the talk. Read the talk through and note the meaning of each section, each idea, each critical term. When you believe you know the talk well, you can move to the next stage, which is discovering the sound of the talk.

The talk begins to come alive as you discover its sound. This can be done only by reading aloud and focusing on the following as you read:

1. Pronounce each syllable of each word. Every word should be heard in its entirety. Don't exaggerate pronunciation; just allow each word its due.

2. Pause at the ends of sentences, at semicolons, at commas, and at other natural breaks in the talk. Learn to adjust your pauses to the content of the talk. Pause longer at the ends of critical ideas than at the ends of supporting or subordinate ideas.

3. Listen for the rhythm of the talk and note how some ideas are— or should be—strongly emphasized, and others are subordinated. Let your voice reinforce rather than resist the rhythm of the talk.

4. Experiment with the sound of the talk by repeating words, sentences, and portions of the talk, with different patterns of stress and emphasis. Continue this process until you feel the appropriate meaning is being conveyed. A tape recorder may be a useful tool at this stage of your preparation. As you listen to the tape of your practice session, ask yourself, "Does that sound oral?" Does the oral interpretation convey the meaning that is intended?

5. Be particularly cautious about the rate of your speaking. Manuscript speaking easily takes on a reading rather than speaking rate. Use the natural pauses in the talk to "brake" your normal tendency toward a reading rate.

When you believe you know the manuscript intimately and can interpret it orally, then you should begin to focus on effective delivery. Your practice should focus on the following guidelines:

1. Stand comfortably but alertly but slightly away from the lectern. You should be close enough to read the manuscript, but you should not hover over it. Your hands may rest lightly on the lectern in a position to slide the manuscript pages to one side as you finish reading from them. Most speakers will place the script slightly to the right of center and then slide pages to the left as they are completed. Don't flip pages or lift them more than is necessary to quietly and unobtrusively slide them out of the way.

2. Discipline yourself to read meaningful groups of words. A major drawback to manuscript speaking is the constant head bobbing that results from brief glances at the script and equally brief glances at the audience members. The result is too often a halting, tortured reading of the script and eye contact that cannot be sustained long enough to be meaningful. To make manuscript speaking work, you must discipline yourself to a different pattern of reading. The new pattern will seem awkward at first, but it will serve you well if you persist.

Look at the script and try to take in a group of words or sentences. The general pattern is for you to look at the manuscript while reading the first part of a sentence, thought unit, or paragraph. When you are confident that you can finish the sentence, thought unit, or paragraph without looking down at the manuscript, look at the audience. Force yourself to sustain this pattern. It is better to continue to read directly from the script for extended periods at the beginning of your practice. Avoid head bobbing and the inevitable and noticeable interruptions in the flow of the talk that result from continually looking from script to audience and rapidly back to the script. Your purpose is to establish and sustain eye contact with the members of your audience. To do this you need to be able to see meaningful groups of words that will stick in your mind as you engage the eyes of your listeners.

Continue this practice until you can look down briefly and then easily finish a couple of sentences, a paragraph, or an entire page. Your goal is to look at your audience approximately 80 percent of the time. Remind yourself that you are attempting to establish and sustain meaningful eye contact with audience members. Do not, however, attempt to memorize. If you find yourself struggling to recall a word or phrase, look at the script and begin to read until you are again confident that you can look up and finish a thought. Remind yourself that the script is right there in front of you; there is no point in struggling to recall a word.

3. Identify places in the script where sustained eye contact with the audience or sustained reading is appropriate or necessary. As you become more familiar with the script, you will discover places where the content demands sustained eye contact or where sustained reading is appropriate or necessary. For example, the first few pages and the last three or four pages are probably more effectively delivered with 100-percent eye contact. Long quotations, statistical information, technical descriptions, or simply parts of the talk you find particularly troublesome, even though they are not particularly critical, may be read in their entirety. Don't struggle over those words, phrases, or sentences that are mysteriously difficult for you. Read from the script when necessary. If you are interpreting the script well, the worst that can result is a brief interruption of eye contact. That is preferable to the awkward interruptions in both the flow of ideas and eye contact if you attempt to fight your way through a portion of the script that persistently and vexingly troubles you.

4. Prepare yourself for appropriate gestures. As you become more familiar with the talk you should find yourself gesturing more often with your hands and arms. Don't plan gestures and don't work to repress them. Relax your hands and arms, focus on your audience and the meaning you are attempting to convey, and let your hands and arms complement your talk. Since you are restricted to the area behind the lectern, your gestures will have to be above the lectern and within a few feet of either side of the lectern. It is appropriate to turn your body to one side or the other and gesture in that direction. Try, however, not to favor any particular segment of the audience, and avoid mechanical sweeps from one side to the other.

I have discovered that practicing to deliver a talk from manuscript requires a different approach from practicing extemporaneous speaking. My bias is for shorter, more efficient practice sessions on a regular basis over a definite period of time. This is especially important when practicing for delivery using a manuscript; it is too easy to begin reading mechanically when you become tired. Make your practice sessions count by following a constructive and efficient practice pattern that will allow you to progress at a steady pace. My recommendation is for two practice sessions each day for a week or so before actual presentation; each practice session should not require more than an hour.

Begin each practice session by reading the manuscript aloud without looking up. The purpose here is to help you become increasingly familiar with the words, ideas, and structure of the speech. By looking at the entire speech as you read, you learn to see it not as a series of single words but as clumps of words and ideas. If your office telephone number is 482-9501, you do not see it as 4–8–2–9–5–0–1. Because you are familiar with it, you are likely to see it as 482–95–01 or even 4829501. Reading the script aloud encourages the same kind of familiarity with words, sentences, or whole pages. Reading the entire manuscript aloud also familiarizes you with the sound and feel of the speech. Such familiarity will help achieve a lively, oral quality in the manuscript presentation.

Now go through the script, reading aloud and focusing on achieving sustained eye contact with the anticipated audience. If you envision the anticipated audience arrayed before you, your practice presentations are apt to be lively. A little imagination doesn't cost much. Again, avoid head bobbing. Discipline yourself to read until you are sure you can look up while finishing at least one thought unit. Use the natural pause at the end of each sentence to look down and begin reading the next line. Avoid interrupting thought units by looking up and down within a thought unit. Work for fluency and meaningful eye contact. Do not repeat any portion of the talk; simply move from beginning to end, even if initially it is rough and awkward.

After you have been through the manuscript two or three times—including the first word-for-word reading—stop. Overpractice is counterproductive. Take a moment or two to assess your progress and plan the next practice session. Perhaps during the next session you will read some portion of the talk differently to more closely reflect your intended meaning. Perhaps you feel confident that you can present the first two minutes of the talk without referring to the script. Jot a note or two to yourself; promise yourself to take advantage of the next regularly scheduled practice; and go about your business assured that you are on your way to an effective presentation.

There is no great mystery to effective speech delivery. Good delivery is intended to complement the message, to reflect directly your efforts to adapt to the requirements and opportunities of each speaking situation. Extemporaneous delivery is especially appropriate for those occasions when spontaneity, flexibility, and direct interaction with audience members are likely to be most effective. Formal situations or situations where precision is important or demanded are situations where manuscript speaking can be used to good effect. As an aspiring public person, you should become proficient at using either extemporaneous delivery or the quarter-sheet manuscript format. Effective speech delivery is not complex; it is guided by a few common-sense principles. But good delivery may be the difference between a poor public speech (or even a good one) and a speech that electrifies an audience and ensures your success.

SUMMARY

Delivery is not a first consideration for effective public communication, but it is an important consideration. A poorly prepared message is rarely saved by good delivery, but good delivery is usually necessary to ensure the effectiveness of well prepared messages. It is also true that the competence of a public speaker will be judged as much by delivery as by the content of the speech. Effective public communicators learn to select the method of delivery to fit the peculiar characteristics of each speaking situation. In most situations, the extemporaneous speech will be appropriate. However, in an increasing number of situations, speeches will require the use of a manuscript. Careful planning and practice can ensure that delivery will be interesting and compelling regardless of the method of delivery used. This chapter has examined such factors of effective delivery as eye contact, body language, vocal qualities, and the handling of audiovisuals. It has stressed the critical importance of practicing your delivery. When delivery is managed well, listeners seem not to notice it; they focus instead on what the speaker says. No effective public communicator should expect more or less of good delivery.

CHAPTER 6

Questions, Answers, and Mandatory Options in Public Communication

Some years ago an American automobile manufacturer produced a new model that was heavily promoted by an extensive advertising campaign. The car came with a number of attractive features described in the advertising as options. But buyers soon learned they could not purchase the car without the so-called options. Salespeople routinely referred to options and "mandatory options"; and they appeared to regard this contradiction in terms as perfectly normal. The practice is no longer permitted.

This chapter addresses the matter of responding to questions in public settings. Often formal presentations are followed by question sessions of varying length; indeed, some presentations are intended to serve only as a preliminary to the real business of the encounter, which is a question-and-answer session. Presidential press conferences are examples of this practice. Sometimes the entire encounter is a question session. At other times questions are only briefly permitted after a presentation. In some particularly informal situations, the speaker may invite and respond to questions which interrupt the presentations.

QUESTION SESSIONS

Question sessions have generally been viewed as the speaker's option. Your decision whether or not to permit questions should be based on your analysis of the requirements of a particular speaking situation. I would suggest that unless there is good reason to the contrary, question sessions   **117** should be considered a mandatory option. Increasingly, audiences expect to be given the opportunity to question speakers after presentations and during presentations. As an aspiring public communicator, you can ill afford to regard question sessions as a nuisance. On the contrary, question sessions ought to be regarded as opportunities to further advance your purpose in speaking. Question sessions can clarify, illustrate, and persuade. Handled well, the question session will enhance the credibility you attempted to establish in the presentation. Question sessions can provide you with invaluable information about the extent to which you have succeeded or failed in public encounters. Viewing question sessions as a mandatory option makes sense; the question session is an opportunity that should be anticipated, eagerly sought, and exploited whenever possible.

There are, of course, some approaches to question sessions which I regard as both adverse to good public communication and ultimately dangerous and costly to those who attempt them. For example, I do not think it makes sense to encourage audience members to ask questions if you cannot or will not answer their questions. I have been amazed and distressed in recent years to discover formal training programs which teach executives techniques for deflecting, avoiding, or confusing questions in public encounters. I recently reviewed printed materials for a nationally prominent training organization that suggested speakers learn to rephrase hostile or difficult questions so that they answer a question they would *rather* have heard—instead of the question asked. I understand that question sessions can be risky and embarrassing, but I see no value in training professional people to be noncommunicative in situations which require effective public communication. As I suggested earlier in this book, nonsense has the ultimately fatal disadvantage of being nonsense. Audiences are not easily fooled.

Preparing for question sessions is much like preparing for a public presentation. You must have a clear idea of what you are attempting to accomplish and a good idea about what the anticipated audience situation will allow and require. Beyond that, you must be well informed. No speaking technique will save you from embarrassment if you do not know what you clearly should know. I attended a conference some time ago and listened to an impressive presentation in which the speaker referred repeatedly to "lag sequential analysis." In the question period that followed, a questioner asked why lag sequential analysis was chosen for use in the research project—a perfectly reasonable question to ask. The speaker was forced to admit that he knew very little about lag sequential analysis, that he had not chosen it for the research, and that he had not conducted or interpreted the results of that portion of the project. The question session promptly ended, leaving the speaker to speculate about the damage done to his credibility. Thorough preparation is critical for public encounters, especially question sessions.

I have spoken earlier and at length about the methods of becoming informed about the subjects you plan to discuss publicly. It is worthwhile to anticipate questions an alert audience might ask in a particular situation. If you put yourself in the role of audience member, you can often generate a list of questions likely to be asked. Practice answering those questions until you feel you can do so accurately, completely, and confidently. If you can manage it, practice the presentation before friends or colleagues and ask them to ask questions following the presentation.

Some months ago, the news media carried stories that aides to President Reagan were concerned about his performances in press conferences. While he handled most presentations with skill, his press conferences were near-disasters. The president sounded tentative and occasionally confused, he got his facts mixed up, and he sometimes became snappish as reporters pursued questions he had handled badly. Interestingly, former President Nixon reportedly encouraged Reagan to set aside several hours to prepare for press conferences. Nixon urged the president to anticipate questions and have his aides do the same and then spend time rehearsing answers to the questions. The media noted improvement in the president's handling of press conferences shortly after the stories of Nixon's recommendation to the president appeared. Rehearsing your answers in anticipation of questions makes as much sense as rehearsing and practicing your speech.

Several characteristics mark the question session and distinguish it from the speech presentation which most often precedes it. The question session is expected to be less formal than the speech presentation. The give-and-take of the question session contrasts sharply with the presentation where the speaker holds the floor for a sustained and structured period. The question period is often not as time-constrained as the presentation. Listeners aren't usually prepared to allow you to speak for more than twenty minutes, but question sessions often run for longer periods of time. As long as members of the audience are interested both in asking questions and listening to others ask questions, and as long as you are not running afoul of some time demands imposed on the situation, it's usually a good idea to continue the question session.

The question session shifts between more or less direct person-to-person interaction and one-to-many interaction. When a member of the audience asks a question, the interaction takes on the qualities of direct person-to-person interaction. Others in the audience may not hear the question, and at least initially that is not a major concern. The questioner is interested primarily in having you hear the question. You must, of course, focus on the questioner to ensure that you hear the entire question with all of its potentially important overtones, and to ensure that you see how the question is being asked. Is the questioner confused or hostile? Does the questioner's tone or body language suggest something of how the questioner feels about the question? Initially, there are qualities that make the interaction more or less direct, person-to-person interaction. Both you and the questioner are aware that other people are present and attending to what is happening, but you and the questioner must, for a brief time, screen out other members of the audience. Some dialogue may take place as you and the questioner attempt to clarify the question. As soon as you believe you have the question the questioner intends, a transformation takes place. Now the question no longer belongs to the questioner or to you: it is on the floor, and it belongs to you and to the entire audience. It is your question to answer, and you do so for the benefit of each member of the audience. Managing this shift in interaction is part of the challenge involved in managing question sessions effectively.

Managing question sessions following a presentation or a question session which represents the entire agenda for a public encounter is largely a matter of control. You must control yourself, the situation, the questioners, and your answers. I will explore each of these areas of control in describing how to manage most question sessions. I will conclude, then, by examining the additional, special requirements you must meet when you engage in interviews or other question sessions attended by or conducted by representatives of the print or electronic media.

Control Yourself

Learning to control public question sessions is first a matter of controlling yourself. I have argued repeatedly in these chapters that self-control or self-discipline is necessary to effective communication in all situations. In responding to questions in public situations, it is essential. Controlling yourself includes physical control and psychological control. You should look relaxed but alert. Where appropriate, smile, but do not force a smile. You should look confident, poised, and eager to engage with your audience. Avoid fidgeting, pacing, hand wringing, and other mannerisms that distract and even irritate your audience. Establish and maintain continuous eye contact with the audience. If possible, move toward questioners while they are asking a question. This conveys a sincere interest in the question and the questioner, and it is likely to be viewed by the audience as an indication of your confidence.

Psychological control simply means remaining calm and cool during the question session. Don't be hurried or attempt to match the hectic pace your listeners may attempt to impose upon you. You may have watched in March 1981, when the news media flashed the news that President Reagan and his press secretary had been shot. Within minutes, reporters converged on the White House pressroom and besieged the assistant press secretary. The pressroom was chaotic with questions being shouted from all quarters. The assistant unfortunately attempted for a time to handle all the questions being fired at him, but his effort quickly collapsed as the task became far too much to handle. He looked confused, distraught, and decidedly unhappy. Maintaining a pace that you control is necessary to success in public question sessions.

Psychological control is also a matter of maintaining a consistent demeanor. Be natural, be yourself, and be consistent. Sudden changes in your demeanor suggest to an audience insincerity and a loss of control. You should not attempt to match occasional hostility or sarcasm of some audience members. We all have witnessed unsightly outbursts by speakers who lose their composure under the pressure of questioning from reporters and others. Such outbursts inevitably result in loss of credibility of the speaker, and little else is remembered of the encounter except the outburst. In most public situations, audience members are on your side or at least willing to hear you out, so long as you don't alienate them by losing your composure. Control yourself and you will control the question session.

Control the Situation

To control the situation, you must set the tone and establish the ground rules for the question session. For example, precede the question period with a few words about the subject areas in which you are prepared to answer questions. You may identify time limitations on the question session and perhaps identify topics you cannot discuss. Usually it is a good idea to provide a succinct justification for your unwillingness or inability to respond to questions about particular matters. "I can't respond to questions about my company's recent rate increase proposal since state law prohibits public discussion while the proposal is being reviewed by the Public Service Commission"; or "I am prepared to discuss company policy, but I'm not qualified to discuss the technical details of our new process."

Controlling the situation may also mean getting the question period started and stimulating audience participation. For any number of reasons, members of the audience may be reluctant to ask the first question. You may end a presentation, ask for questions, and hear the audience go silent. It's awkward, but it does not necessarily mean the members of the audience have no questions. It may mean that each member of the audience is reluctant to start. Two techniques can be attempted. First, you can simply wait out the audience for a few moments. Stop talking, look at the audience as if you expect a question, and wait. Your silence may be just the stimulus needed for some person in the audience to ask the first question. Once the first question has been asked, other questions are likely to follow.

A second technique to get the question period started is the use of stock questions. In preparing for the question session you should have generated a number of potential questions. Select from these a few questions which you feel touch upon common audience concerns, likely to provoke other questions. For example, a speaker who has just completed a demonstration and discussion of a microcomputer and its peripherals may say, "When I have demonstrated this equipment before business people like you, one of the first questions I get is, 'How much does all that cost?' " After answering his or her own question, the speaker says, "Perhaps you have some questions about cost that I haven't touched upon, or perhaps you have other questions." You may also wish to ask a more open-ended question. For example, "Are there areas of concern I did not touch upon in my presentation that you feel I might help you with?" These techniques are intended to stimulate an audience to ask questions. If you cannot provoke a question after a couple of attempts, don't press further. Thank the audience for the opportunity to speak with them about your topic and close the encounter. Your task is to control the situation, not to imprison a reluctant or even a dead audience.

Control the Questioner

Controlling the question session also means controlling the questioner. This does not mean that you must dominate the question session or that you must intimidate questioners. It does mean that you must work constantly to make the question session understandable and satisfying for the *entire* audience, and that you must use the session as another opportunity to achieve your purposes through interaction with the audience. Question sessions pose a serious risk. If you do not exert some control over those who ask questions, they may seize the opportunity to control the audience for their own purposes. Any company president who has conducted an annual stockholders' meeting is aware of this risk. If not controlled, a questioner may become a competing speaker. Because this risk is particularly troublesome, I will deal with it at some length by describing in detail how you respond to a question from the audience from the moment the questioner is recognized and begins to speak.

Controlling the questioner begins by carefully watching and listening as the question is being asked. Concentrate intently on the questioner. Don't let yourself be distracted. Listen to the question to determine its content, its emotional overtones, and its contextual features. The content refers to the information being sought. If I ask, "How old are you?" it is pretty clear what kind of information will be needed to answer the question. The emotional overtones, which are conveyed largely by nonverbal clues, complicate the question a bit. These overtones tell us if the question is friendly, hostile, or neutral. Facial expressions, posture, gestures, and vocal qualities, along with the question content, reveal the emotional state of the questioner who asks the question.

The contextual features of a question refer to how the question describes past, present, and future events. Questions don't occur in a vacuum. They have histories, they occur at a particular moment in the present, and they point to the future. To understand the contextual features of a question is to understand where it is coming from, how it fits in the present, and where it is going. Note the contextual features in this question posed for a corporate officer: "You said two years ago that this company would control 40 percent of the domestic market in less than two years. Your current report shows that we have lost 5 percent of the domestic market and now show a 31 percent share. What do you propose to do to recapture what was lost and to increase our share of the domestic market?" Listening to a question for contextual features is a matter of attempting to understand the complete perspective of the questioner so your answer will be as complete as necessary.

Further, understanding contextual features may permit you to avoid being led into an unproductive discussion or a nasty trap. A bank president, presiding at a stockholders' meeting, explained prior to the question session that he was not free to discuss two lawsuits pending against the bank. During the question session, a questioner asked, "What projections do you have concerning legal costs during the next fiscal year?" To answer the question directly would have revealed information about the pending legal actions that the president had refused to discuss earlier and possibly would have led to still more probing into the particulars of the two cases. Recognizing the contextual features of the question and the hazard they posed, the president replied, "I'm sorry I can't talk about legal costs without discussing the two cases pending against the bank, and I have been advised by our legal counsel to avoid public discussion of those cases until they are resolved." Answering questions is a little like driving a car. You need to be alert to where you are, what's behind you, and what's ahead.

Concentrate upon the questioner. While the question is being asked, don't rehearse your answer. Your first task is to be sure you understand the question being asked. When the questioner finishes, you may wish to repeat or restate the question. While this may be awkward and inappropriate when addressing a small group, it is particularly necessary in dealing with large audiences, and it may be useful when the question is unclear to you or to others in the audience.

Repeating or restating a question gives you control of it. By merely providing the audience with an opportunity to hear the question or by restating it in clearer language, you take control of it. Now it's your question to answer fully and clearly for the benefit of the entire audience. Some questions are confusing. The questioner may be a little embarrassed, and unsure of how to ask the question. After his verbal stumbling, the question may emerge but in an unclear form. When you rephrase the question you help the questioner as well as the audience. Your ability to make something worthwhile of a verbal farrago will very likely be noticed and appreciated by the audience.

Of course, you must try to avoid misstating the question that was asked. If you can do so without getting bogged down, ask the questioner if your restatement of the question is correct. If nothing else, this indicates to the questioner and to the audience that you are sincerely interested in answering *their* questions, not your version of their questions. As a further check, when you complete the answer you may wish to ask the questioner if you have answered the question. This, of course, does not mean you must dedicate the entire question session to attempts to understand all the nuances of a single question. Good judgment will allow you to know when further efforts at clarification are useless and when it's time to entertain another question from a different questioner. You want to be fair without being obsequious; your responsibility is to the entire audience, and so long as the audience's needs and interests as well as your own are being served by attempting to clarify a question, it is time well spent.

Occasionally questions are hopelessly ambiguous, or clearly loaded, or complex, or incomprehensible. Some simple techniques, used *before* attempting an answer, will help you manage these kinds of questions and retain control of the questioners. Some questioners, for example, may try to confuse you with a long, rambling, and ambiguous question. Or the questioner may be confused, and the result is a long, rambling, mess of a question. The easiest response is to turn the question back to the questioner. Ask him to clarify his own question. This simple technique often produces startling results. Ask the questioner to restate the question, or say, "What is your question?" If the questioner persists with a confusing question, try restating the question for yourself and the audience. For example, you can say, "If I understand what you are asking, it is this. . . ." State the question as best you can, answer it as well as you can, and then move on to another question. A major rule for managing question sessions is that you should never attempt to answer a question you do not understand.

Some questions are loaded: questioners may attempt to force a kind of "have-you-stopped-beating-your-wife" question upon you. A telephone company employee speaking about measured service was asked by an obviously overwrought questioner, "When is your company going to stop using your clout with the Public Service Commission to rip off old people living on fixed incomes?" This is a loaded question. Words like *clout* and expressions like *rip off* are the hallmarks of emotion-laden questions. There is little value in responding in kind to this kind of invective; you will gain little by engaging in an argument with such a questioner. A better approach is to search for the issues or concerns that underlie the question. You may wish to share the underlying concern without agreeing with the conclusion suggested by the question. In this case, the issues are the costs of telephone service—particularly to senior citizens living on fixed incomes and the way rates are set by a regulatory body. Your answer should address these issues. The telephone company employee answered the question by first identifying with the concern: "We are concerned about the impact of increased costs for telephone services upon people with fixed incomes. Inflation hurts these people the most. Our rate increases, however, have been substantially below the rate of inflation over the past twelve years; we're trying to hold the line against the effects of inflation." The answer then dealt with the issue concerning the way rates are set. "Our rates are set by an independently selected government body established by law to serve the public interest. I believe most people who have watched the Public Service Commission in recent years will agree that the commission has done a good job of representing the public interest." Loaded questions require poise, patience, and the willingness to look for interests and concerns amid the verbal fire and smoke.

Complex questions make it difficult for you to remain in control of the question session. The complexity of a question may make it difficult to answer completely, and the questioner may be expected to press for an answer to any portion of the question left unanswered. From time to time a question which apparently invites a simple "Yes" or "No" requires a more complex and qualified response. Two techniques can be recommended. First, don't be in a hurry to say "Yes" or "No" to a question. If you have been listening for the context as well as the content and emotion in the questions, you are more likely to detect the hazards in a too-facile "Yes" or "No" response. It is often difficult to get audience members to listen carefully to the qualifications that follow a "Yes" or "No" response. For many, "Yes" or "No" represents a final and definitive response that relieves listeners of the need to listen further. So get the qualifications up front. Don't say, "Yes, that's true if you understand that. . . ." Say instead, "If you understand that . . . then the answer could be Yes." In this way you provide audience members with an appreciation of the necessary complexity that may underlie apparently simple matters.

Next, you can respond to complex questions and control the questioner by previewing the organization of your answer. When you say, for example, "There are two points I'd like to make in response to that question," you have effectively prevented the questioner from interrupting your complete response. Further, you have assisted the other audience members by structuring what is for them complex and, therefore, difficult to follow. You need not, of course, be constrained by the way the questioner has framed a question. What is presented to you as one question may be several questions requiring different answers. Again, control the question and the questioner by previewing the organization of your response. You can say, "There are three questions in what you've asked. I'll answer the third one first and then tackle the first and second in order." Previewing the structure of your response requires careful listening, organizational ability, and the poise to resist being manipulated or confused by a questioner.

Finally, you control the questioner by preventing any single questioner from monopolizing a question session. Most often a questioner will monopolize a question session not because of some malevolent intent but because of keen interest or an aggressive personal style. There is no point in attempting to embarrass or intimidate such people. A more benign but effective technique works as well. Move toward the questioner while you are being asked the question and concentrate upon the question being asked. Be sure you understand the question and by your actions evince a willingness to give the questioner a complete opportunity to ask a question. Once you begin to answer the question, however, direct your attention to the entire audience. Move away from the questioner to a point more central to the full audience. When you have finished your answer, look toward a segment of the audience away from the previous questioner and say, "Let me give the people over here a chance to ask some questions. Did I see a hand up over here?" If a single questioner persists in efforts to attract your attention while you are trying to give other audience members a chance to ask questions, you can say, "You have a number of questions to ask that I'd like to answer. But I want to give others a chance to ask questions, too. Perhaps you and I can talk after the session." You are expected to control the question session, and most audience members will appreciate your efforts to direct the verbal traffic so that it flows more evenly and smoothly.

Control Your Answers

Finally, to control the question session you must control your answers. Be as succinct as you can manage while answering the question completely. But answer only the question that was asked. Organize your answers so that audience members can follow them more easily. Where possible, illustrate, amplify, and support your answers with fresh materials. Use the same language in the question session that you would use in presenting a speech. Don't use technical language or jargon when it is possible to use simple, more direct language. Be as direct, as interesting, and as succinct as you can manage.

Control your answers, too, by developing a public orientation. Your answers should respond to the audience's needs, concerns, and interests. If you are a business person, you should understand that most audience members are not interested in the internal difficulties of your company. They are interested in how your operations affect their interests and needs. Chester Burger provides an example of how a question can be made to reflect a public orientation:

[D]uring negotiations for a new contract, corporate spokesmen will tell the press, in effect, "We can't afford the increase the union is asking." That may be true, but why should the public be concerned with the company's financial problems? Employees often respond with hostility and resentment. It is much better to say, "We'd like to give our employees the increase they seek. But if our costs go up too much, our customers won't buy. That will hurt us, and in the end, it will endanger our employees' jobs."[1]

A spokesperson for the telephone company may argue that competition in the telecommunications industry will hurt profits. But the public is more likely to respond favorably if the company spokesperson says instead:

We are for competition when it serves the public interest as well as our own. But we have provided some customer services at prices below our costs for those services. We could do that because we were permitted to make enough money on some other services to offset those losses. Competition, however, drives all prices toward cost. If telecommunication services are to be offered in a completely competitive environment, then we could compete and do well. But some services, like residential telephone service, will have to be priced closer to their actual cost. That means your home telephone service will cost more to use, while long distance charges will be less expensive.

Be careful, of course, not to overdo your efforts to sustain a public orientation. It is often useful to admit your self-interest, especially when your self-interest also serves the public interest. A local manufacturing company recently installed expensive sewage-treatment equipment in one of its plants. When asked if this was done because of concern for the local environment, the company spokesperson replied, "We are interested in preserving the environment, but beyond that these new facilities allow us to recover a number of useful by-products of our manufacturing process which were previously wasted." Admitting self-interest is likely to make statements of concern for public interests more credible.

You can control your answer, too, by developing and using a theme. The residual message from your speech may allow you to organize your answers to a number of questions and demonstrate the consistency of your responses. Examples of theme statements include "Competition drives prices toward cost," "Public service does not mean poor or overpriced service," "Education is much cheaper than ignorance," and "Business and government are much better as partners than as competitors." A good theme will allow you to defeat efforts to confuse you, to shift ground in the questioning, and to force you out of a consumer orientation. Use the theme to keep the questions and your responses focused on the area of your greatest preparation.

You control your answers, too, if you learn when and how to say, "I don't know." Knowing when to say you don't know is easy. If you don't know the answer to a question, if you know only a part of the answer, or if you can only guess at an answer, you are better off admitting you don't know the answer. Often a partial answer may be unsatisfactory, particularly if the questioner's major concern is left unanswered. Knowing how to say you don't know is critical in controlling the question session. It is perfectly acceptable to say, "I'm sorry, my training is in the application of computers to manufacturing processes. I can't answer your question about the use of microcomputers in the dairy industry."

Your credibility is not likely to suffer if you admit that what you know may not be helpful to a questioner. You may say, for example, "I know a bit about microcomputers, but I don't have enough expertise to help you with that particular question." Or you can say, "I don't have enough information to answer your question, and I don't want to confuse the issue." Remember, public audiences do not expect you to know everything.

A technique successfully employed by a number of business and professional people is to admit ignorance of the matter and offer to assist the questioner in finding the answer. This should be done without evaluating the question. If you say, "That's a good question," you imply that others were not so good or that the only good questions are the ones you can't answer. It is better to say, "I don't know the answer to that question, but I would like to know it, and I would like to find it out for you. Let me have your name and telephone number after the program and I'll get back to you with an answer within two days." Of course, there is no value in making such promises publicly if you are not prepared to keep them.

Finally, in controlling your answers remember that nothing is off the record in public encounters. You will be held accountable for what you say and how you say it. Suggesting in response to a question that your answer is "off the record" or "not for public information" is a risky business at best. You are better advised to assume that what you say will be repeated and attributed to you. If it is truly confidential, don't say it in public.

This of course does not cover everything there is to know about answering questions in public sessions. I have tried to provide some key ideas to assist your preparation for question sessions and some specific techniques to use in particularly troublesome situations. You can learn to be effective in answering questions if you learn to control yourself, control the situation, control the questioner, and control your responses. Control is the key to effectiveness in all question sessions. There are, however, additional requirements that you must meet when you are questioned by the media. This chapter will conclude by focusing on those special concerns and requirements.

RESPONDING TO THE MEDIA

Increasingly, executives and managers in both the public and private sectors have found it necessary to respond to questions in public forums and through the media. The "public's right to know" has been extended to include virtually all activities by private corporations, major industries, and public agencies. There is little value in either lauding or lamenting this relatively recent development; it is a fact. The concern is to respond as effectively as possible when it becomes necessary to do so. In most instances, public question sessions represent opportunities to disseminate information, clarify issues, correct misinformation, and even advocate particular positions. And in most instances the media facilitate these legitimate public goals. Occasionally, however, the media may take an adversary or even hostile position toward you, toward the positions you represent, or toward both. When that occurs, it is necessary to know how to handle yourself and how to achieve your ends, despite the obstacles that hostile or cynical media may create for you. The suggestions made here, together with those made earlier, are intended to assist you in responding effectively to the media.

Keep first things first. Public forums are rarely done just for the media. Most often the media are seen as the most effective way of reaching a larger public—perhaps specific publics. You must consequently concentrate upon the unseen audience behind the microphones, cameras, and reporters' notepads. Speak to that other audience. As often as you can, respond to what you consider to be their perspectives, their levels of understanding, their experiences, their interests, and their concerns. Speak in personal terms, using "I" and "we" and "you" as often as possible. Envision that broader audience as specifically as you can.

As with any question session, establish and maintain your own pace. Occasionally, it is to the advantage of media interviewers to push you along as fast as they can. Reporters like to pack a lot of information into a short period of time. Sometimes a hurried response makes juicy news. Consequently, set your own pace and refuse to dance to the frantic music that some media folk will play for you. You are not obligated to fill space for reporters; don't be in a hurry to answer any question, even those questions you like to answer. Don't speak before you are ready to speak.

Most people have very little experience in managing microphones, television cameras, studio lighting, and other tools and trappings familiar to the electronic media. Because of their inexperience, they often feel awkward and a bit victimized when confronted with such paraphernalia. To make matters worse, reporters and interviewers often ask you to accommodate yourself to the limitations imposed by such equipment. The following suggestions are intended to assist you in avoiding such situations:

1. In public interviews focus your attention on the interviewer. When you are being interviewed before an audience, focus your attention on the audience as you respond to questions, but look at the interviewer as you are being questioned. Do not be bullied into looking into a particular camera, speaking into a particular microphone, etc. Adapt an attitude of blissful ignorance of such technical matters and concentrate on effective communication. Whether they indicate it to you or not, studio technicians are paid to adapt their equipment to assist you in being effective with the audience.

2. Be particularly wary of reporters who attempt to get you to follow a moving microphone. Often the microphone is withdrawn before you've finished an answer, or it is pushed toward your face before you expect it. Simple courtesy is not universally accepted among media reporters. The remedy: Ignore the microphone. Don't answer until you're ready; and once you've begun, simply continue speaking—with vigorous projection—until you've finished. Don't filibuster, but don't allow your answers to be cut short.

3. When a reporter insists that you adapt to the equipment, simply politely decline to continue the question session or interview—or better, decline to begin. There is nothing that says you must be uncomfortable or look and feel awkward in public forums in order to accommodate the media.

4. In a talk show interview on television, concentrate on the interviewer or host. The format is usually intended to simulate informal conversation in a "living-room" setting. Behave as you would in a friend's home. Do not try to look into the "right" camera or into the lights. Let the technicians worry about such details, and let them accommodate the equipment to you.

5. Finally, and most importantly, establish the ground rules in advance. The media session requires you to control the situation as you would other question sessions. Ask about the general areas to be covered, indicate areas where you will not respond to questions or cannot respond, ask about the length of the interview, and inquire about the opportunity to retape or otherwise correct any misstatements you might make in a free-wheeling interview situation. If you are uncomfortable with the ground rules, decline the interview and tell the newspaper, radio station, or television station management directly and in writing why you have declined and the conditions you will accept. Don't be overly rigid. Establish reasonable guidelines for yourself, but don't permit yourself to be intimidated.

The content of media sessions must be managed as you would expect to manage the content of any question session. Refer to the earlier discussion of how to control the questioner. It is important to understand questions before answering them, to provide qualifications before a "Yes" or "No" response, and to know when and how to say, "I don't know." It is particularly important not to argue with a reporter or interviewer. If the reporter or interviewer becomes rude and boorish, you should remain cool and pleasant. The audience will more easily side with you. Remember, too, that the interviewer has the advantage of editing; a nasty or outrageous question can be edited out, and only the irritated response left.

Of course, do not lie, exaggerate, or speak facetiously in media sessions. What you say constitutes a public record. Even when it is painful to do so, speak the truth. Anything less is excessively expensive in the end.

Finally, look for every opportunity to cooperate with the legitimate operation of the media. Where it is possible for you to interact with media representatives in an atmosphere of mutual respect and concern, do your utmost to respond. Do not assume initially that the media are your enemies. Your approach should be businesslike and cooperative. In most instances the media will be more than happy to accommodate you and provide you with opportunities to have your say. Learn, too, to respond to effective work by media representatives in writing. Often a note to a reporter or interviewer, with a copy to the station management, in which you compliment the reporter on the professionalism demonstrated in a public question session will serve to enhance mutual respect—if not consistent agreement.

SUMMARY

A question session is often the "mandatory option" that follows a public presentation, or it may be the reason for a public encounter. If you understand what a question session requires of you, you should manage it effectively and smoothly. Your task is to control the question session, not in the sense of dominating or unilaterally manipulating for your purposes; rather, you should work to ensure that the question session is useful and satisfying to the audience as well as to you. Media sessions require attention to particular aspects and proclivities of the print and electronic media. Any question session is an opportunity to serve audience interests and needs as well as your own.

Note

1. Burger, C., "How to Meet the Press," *Harvard Business Review* (July–August 1975): 64.

INDEX